C.S. LEWIS GOES to HEAVEN
A Reader's Guide to THE GREAT DIVORCE

BY DAVID G. CLARK

C.S. LEWIS GOES TO HEAVEN:
A Reader's Guide to The Great Divorce

Copyright © 2012 David G. Clark

Winged Lion Press
Hamden, CT

Winged Lion Press titles may be purchased for business or promotional use or special sales.

Cover art and interior illustrations by
Deborah Wilson Camp camp1138@gmail.com

10-9-8-7-6-5-4-3-2-1

WINGED LION PRESS

ISBN 13   978-1-936294-09-1

DEDICATION

This guide to *The Great Divorce* is dedicated to the hundreds of students who took my C. S. Lewis classes over the past three decades. We enjoyed many lively discussions together, followed by boisterous potlucks in memory of the banquet at the Tempter's Training College. Learning flowed in both directions, and our theology was enriched, thanks to Lewis and the inquiring minds who blessed my classrooms. One book posed a greater challenge to us than any other by Lewis, and this dedication introduces my humble attempt to put into words the insights we gained over the years. It is my sincere wish that now *The Great Divorce* will get the respect, and enjoyment, it has long deserved.

ACKNOWLEDGEMENTS

I would be remiss if I failed to express my appreciation for those who have generously offered their assistance over the past few years. First, Rose, whose research, worthy of any detective, helped me unravel a knotty problem or two regarding the ghosts Lewis met on his most unusual journey. Christine Colbert and Lawrence Macala were kind enough to read my efforts and offered many improvements. I salute Terry Lindvall who (in a surprising lapse of good judgment) has written kind words about both of my Lewis books. Debbie Camp opened wonderful windows into the discussions with her illustrations. And I must mention Walter Hooper who provided invaluable assistance to me (and many others, I am sure) via his collected letters of Lewis-what a gigantic task! I consulted the three volumes many times and found much profit therein.

And of course this book would not have seen the light of day if Robert Trexler, publisher of Winged Lion Press, was not willing to take a chance on me. He has patiently coped with all of my questions and last-minute changes. Finally, I scarcely can imagine where I would be without the support of my wife. It's not easy living with a theologian for more than forty years, but she has pulled it off in style. Thank you Sylvia!

CONTENTS

⌘ X ⌘

LEWIS' WORKS

Notes: When only a page number is given with no source in a reference, the edition of *The Great Divorce* cited below is always the referent. References to the other Lewis books listed here will include the abbreviations for those books as well as the page(s) cited. Entries for Lewis books include the date of the edition used here and, in parentheses, the date of original publication. All references to Dante's *Comedy (Commedia)* will be taken from Dorothy Sayers' translation and notes unless otherwise indicated. Therefore, her name has not been cited in the *Comedy* references. But I do cite the work (*Hell, Purgatory** or *Paradise)*, the number of the Canto, the number of the line(s), and the page(s) in the edition cited below. Over the years, Lewis used different formats to indicate the dates of his letters; and the same is true of various editions of the correspondence of other authors I have cited. For clarity and uniformity I have indicated the dates in all correspondence as follows: May 2, 1955.

AMR   *All My Road Before Me: The Diary of C. S. Lewis, 1922-1927*. Walter Hooper, ed. San Diego: Harcourt Brace Jovanovich, A Harvest /HBJ Book, 1991.

CR   *Christian Reflections*. Walter Hooper, ed. Grand Rapids: Eerdmans, 1975 (1967).

CLI   *The Collected Letters of C. S. Lewis*. Vol. I: *Family Letters 1905-1931*. Walter Hooper, ed. HarperSanFrancisco: HarperCollins Publishers, Inc., 2004.

CLII   *The Collected Letters of C. S. Lewis*. Vol. II: *Books, Broadcasts, and the War, 1931-1949*. Walter Hooper, ed. HarperSanFrancisco: HarperCollins Publishers, Inc., 2004.

CLIII   *The Collected Letters of C. S. Lewis*. Vol. III: *Narnia, Cambridge, and Joy, 1950-1963*. Walter Hooper, ed. HarperSanFrancisco: HarperCollins Publishers, Inc., 2007.

EL   *English Literature in the Sixteenth Century Excluding Drama. The Oxford History of English Literature*. Oxford: At the Clarendon Press, 1954.

FL   *The Four Loves*. A Harvest Book. San Diego: Harcourt Brace & Co., 1988 (1960).

GD   *The Great Divorce : A Dream*. A Touchstone Book. New York: Simon & Schuster, 1996 (1946).

GID *God in the Dock. Essays on Theology and Ethics.* Walter Hooper, ed. Grand Rapids: Eerdmans, 2001 (1979).

L *Letters of C. S. Lewis.* Revised and Enlarged Edition. Walter Hooper, ed. A Harvest Book. San Diego: Harcourt Brace & Co, 1993 (1966).

LAL *Letters to An American Lady* (Mary Willis Shelburne). Clyde S. Kilby, ed. Grand Rapids: Eerdmans, 1967.

LB *The Last Battle.* New York: Collier Books, 1977 (1956).

LTM *Letters to Malcolm: Chiefly on Prayer.* San Diego: Harvest/HBJ, 1964.

M *Miracles: A Preliminary Study.* New York: Macmillan, 1965 (1947).

MC *Mere Christianity.* Collier Books, New York: Macmillan, 1960 (1952).

OTW *Of Other Worlds.* Walter Hooper, ed. New York: A Harvest/HJB Book, Harcourt Brace Jovanovich, 1966.

P *Poems.* Walter Hooper, ed. A Harvest Book. New York: Harcourt Brace and Co., 1992 (1964).

PER *Perelandra.* New York: Scribner, 2003 (1944).

PP *The Problem of Pain.* Collier Books. New York: Macmillan, 1962 (1940).

SBJ *Surprised by Joy: The Shape of My Early Life.* New York: Harvest/Harcourt Brace Jovanovich, 1955.

SL & SPT *The Screwtape Letters with Screwtape Proposes a Toast.* Revised Edition, New York: Collier Books, Macmillan, 1982 (1942).

THS *That Hideous Strength.* New York: Scribner Paperback, Simon & Schuster, 1996 (1945).

TWHF *Till We Have Faces: A Myth Retold.* A Harvest Book. San Diego: Harcourt Brace & Co, 1984 (1956).

WG *The Weight of Glory and Other Addresses.* San Francisco: HarperCollins, Zondervan Pub. House, 2001 (1949).

WLN *The World's Last Night and Other Essays.* A Harvest Book. New York: Harcourt Brace Jovanovich, Inc., 1973 (1952).

Books of the Bible

Gen	Genesis
Exo	Exodus
Lev	Leviticus
Num	Numbers
Deut	Deuteronomy
2 Chron	2 Chronicles
Psa	Psalms
Isa	Isaiah
Joel	
Dan	Daniel
Matt	Matthew
Mark	
Luke	
John	
Acts	
Rom	Romans
1 Cor	1 Corinthians
2 Cor	2 Corinthians
Eph	Ephesians
Phil	Philippians
Col	Colossians
1 Thess	1 Thessalonians
2 Thess	2 Thessalonians
1 Tim	1 Timothy
2 Tim	2 Timothy
Heb	Hebrews
James	
1 Pet	1 Peter
2 Pet	2 Peter
1 John	
Jude	
Rev	Revelation

Scripture citations are from the Revised Standard Version in the main text and the New Revised Standard Version in the appendices unless indicated otherwise as follows:

RSV – Revised Standard Version
NRSV – New Revised Standard Version
DC – translation by David Clark.

DEFINITIONS OF THEOLOGICAL TERMS

(Words marked with an asterisk* are described in Appendix IV)

Hades: the Greek word for the abode of the souls of the dead. See also Sheol below. There are several important developments in the theology of Hades in the New Testament compared to earlier Old Testament theology. The souls of the righteous and unrighteous are depicted as waiting in different parts of Hades. Suffering or bliss have already begun and souls are depicted as fully conscious. Finally, as a result of Christ's descent into Hades and his resurrection from the tomb, he now has the "keys of (authority over) death and Hades" (Rev 1:18), and will one day reunite the souls and resurrected bodies of his own. Hades is therefore no longer a permanent prison of the soul.

Heaven: Often means the sky in scripture. Genesis 2:19 refers to the birds of Heaven and James 5:12 speaks of rain from Heaven. The word may also correspond to "space," as in Mark 13:25 where Jesus speaks of stars falling from Heaven. The most familiar meaning in Scripture would be the dwelling place of God and angels. Paul tells the Corinthians that he was caught up (Heaven is always "up" in the Bible) to the third Heaven; i.e., past the sky and space and into the spirit world.

Hell: The final abode of those who refuse Heaven. In Jude, the state of the lost is "deepest darkness" (Jude 13), but the more familiar description of Hell is the lake of fire (Rev 20:11-15), created for Satan and his angels (Matt 25:41).

Justification: The imputation of righteousness to a person, especially in the writings of Paul. By faith Abraham believed the promise of God that he would have descendants and because of that faith, God considered Abraham to be righteous (Gen 15:6). In Christian theology, God imputes righteousness to those who believe that Christ died for their sins (Rom 4:23-25).

Paradise*: Literally, a garden or orchard. In the Septuagint (the Old Testament in Greek) and the Vulgate (Latin) translations, the Garden of Eden is called the Paradise of Eden. *Paradiso* (Paradise) is the title Dante* gave to the third volume of his Comedy, and his Paradise is both the garden from which Adam and Eve were ejected and the outskirts of Heaven. Dante places his Paradise on the top of Mount Purgatory. From there, Dante must ascend through ten levels of Heaven until he finally catches a brief glimpse of the Godhead.

Lewis does not use the word "Paradise," but Dante's Paradise at the top of Purgatory and leading into the lowest Heaven strongly influenced his description of Heaven as a pastoral Paradise. Those who arrive on the bus reach only the "outskirts" of Heaven as in Dante. They do experience a beautiful landscape all around them, but "deep" Heaven is above the mountains in the distance, farther up than the eye can see. They find the density and sharpness of everything uncomfortable, but if they yield to Heaven, they will become "solid" (real) themselves as their souls are cleansed, and be able to "journey" deeper into Heaven or "the High Countries" (10). Thus, as the place of purification, Paradise is Purgatory, which will eventually become Heaven.

Purgatory: Literally, the place of purging; that is, the removal of sins that still remain in the soul after death. In *The Great Divorce*, the drab, monotonous grey town is the place where those who are avoiding God choose to live. Thus, as the place where purification is refused, the grey town will eventually become Hell. When Christ returns with judgment, the bus stop will disappear and only Heaven or Hell will exist. Until then, those who wish (and are still able) can journey on the bus to Paradise/Heaven. If they return to the grey town, they have chosen Hell. If they stay in Heaven, as they reflect on their lives the grey town will have been Purgatory, and so the "outskirts" of Heaven. In fact, this will also be true of the earth, where Heaven and Hell both begin (11, 67).

Lewis emphasizes that the sinful aspects of the soul must die in order for souls to be reborn into what God intended them to be, and the process will be more difficult if a person lived a sinful earthly life. His uncomplicated view of Purgatory is best understood as the continuation of a person's earthly sanctification. If someone who has chosen Heaven is not perfected before death, and if perfection of the soul is necessary for fellowship with a holy God, the doctrine of some kind of Purgatory becomes a logical necessity. Because this doctrine speaks to the consummation of sanctification it has been a part of Christian theology since the first millenium, referred to specifically by this name by Pope Gregory the Great in the 6th century.

Lewis strongly disagreed with many depictions of Purgatory that arose after Dante. In his fictitious correspondence to Malcolm, Lewis noted that in Thomas More's *Supplication of Souls*, Purgatory is simply a temporary Hell. Here the souls are tormented by devils, whose presence is 'more horrible and grievous to us than is the pain itself.' Lewis also takes issue with Fisher, who in his Sermon on Psalm VI, says the tortures are so intense that the spirit who suffers them cannot, for pain, 'remember God as he ought to do.' (LTM: 108)

In such views, Purgatory has become a place of punishment, not purification. Fortunately they do not have the last word on the subject. "The right view returns magnificently in Newman's *Dream*. There, if I remember it rightly, the saved soul, at the very foot of the throne, begs to be taken away and cleansed. It cannot bear for a moment longer 'With its darkness to confront that light.' Religion has reclaimed Purgatory." (LTM: 108)

Sanctification: in the Old Testament, a "setting apart" of something for restricted use. The Mosaic Law required the first-born of flocks and herds to be "set apart" (sacrificed) for God as a reminder to Israel that the angel of God took the lives of the first-born sons of Egypt when God delivered them from bondage (Exo 13:11-16). Even vessels were "set apart" or restricted for temple service, meaning they could not be used for household cooking. This definition does not address moral quality.

This meaning is also used in some New Testament passages, but a second meaning also begins to appear: the removal of sins and the sinful nature from a person's life. Justification speaks to the forgiveness of sins and the believer's being regarded as righteous by God, while sanctification as I shall use the term in this book signifies the process whereby God, with human cooperation and effort, purifies and transforms the soul.

Lewis shared this view of sanctification and even used that theological term in his correspondence. Taking Paul's epistles as his guide, he described it as "the process of 'Christ being formed in us,' the process of becoming like Christ... And no doubt sanctification wd. be the correction both of our congenital or original *sinfulness* and of our actual particular sins" (CLII, "To Edward T. Dell," May 26, 1949; 940.).

Sheol: the Hebrew word for the dwelling place of souls after physical death. See also Hades above. In English translations of the Old Testament, Sheol is sometimes (misleadingly) translated as "grave" or even "Hell." Sheol is often referred to as the "pit" in the Old Testament (Job 17:13-14; Jonah 2:2, 6). Sheol was thought to be a dark and gloomy place, and souls were described in the Old Testament as "shades" or weak shadows of former personalities.

Spirit World: The expression I shall use to include all of the "places," whether "up" or "down" in scripture, that are outside the physical universe: Hades, Tartarus, Paradise, Purgatory, Hell, Heaven, etc.

Tartarus: In late Jewish belief, the very lowest compartment of the underworld where the angels who came down and married women in the time of Noah are imprisoned. In 2 Pet 2:4 they are held there by "chains of darkness" until the day of judgment. In Greek mythology, the Titans (the twelve gods born to Uranus and Gaia) who rebelled against Zeus are imprisoned there.

"Winnowing of Hell:" "Winnowing" is the process of tossing grain such as wheat into the air with a basket, shovel or fork to let the wind separate the kernels from the chaff. John the Baptist described Christ as holding a winnowing fork in his hand; i.e., ready to bring judgment. In church tradition, the phrase refers to Christ's descending into Hades after His crucifixion, bringing out from there the souls that belong to Him, and leading them into Paradise, a new place in the Spirit World He has prepared for His own. In *The Great Divorce*, Lewis depicts this change of places as souls taking a bus ride.

FOREWORD

The Great Divorce (GD) first came before the public in weekly installments as "Who Goes Home" or "The Grand Divorce," published by *The Guardian*, from November 1944 through April 1945. But the Anglican newspaper was not the only voice for Clive Staples Lewis during these two years. *Beyond Personality* also appeared in 1944, plus eighteen articles in a variety of magazines, and the first eight installments of "Who Goes Home." In 1945 *That Hideous Strength* and sixteen articles on a variety of topics were published, plus the remaining fifteen installments of "Who Goes Home." Finally, in January 1946, the twenty-three installments were published in book form as *The Great Divorce*. (Hooper, *C. S. Lewis*: 804-5, 823-828).

Clearly, Lewis was in his prime during the war years, being in his midforties. *The Screwtape Letters* began to appear weekly in 1941 (also in *The Guardian*), and this imaginary correspondence reveals his preoccupation with the fragility of human life. Not only did the aggressors of World War II threaten civilization itself, mankind must also struggle against temptations of all sorts devised by sinister beings of the spirit world.

Lewis was also profoundly interested in the condition of souls between death and the resurrection, as many of his writings show. After all, the choices souls make there, and back on earth, eventually lead to one of two possible destinations. To explore human existence in the intermediate state, and also what Christ accomplished when He descended into Hades, Lewis decided to go there himself, as did Dante before him, and Virgil* before Dante.

It is not surprising then, that GD is a summation of these and other theological issues that Lewis was working through since his conversion more than a decade ago. Add to his theology a rich background in mythology, his enjoyment of and deep familiarity with Dante and Milton,* the impact of the revelations of Julian* of Norwich, to mention just a few influences, and the result is one of the most powerful expressions of the twentieth century of an outstanding intellect at the height of its powers.

An interesting anecdote from someone who had the opportunity to speak to Lewis about GD shows that he found personal satisfaction in what he had written. On Friday, July 20, 1956, Kathryn Lindskoog met with Lewis and his brother Warren for some seventy-five minutes at the Royal Oxford Hotel. When she commented that *The Great Divorce* was her favorite book of his, Lewis was pleased and said that it was his "Cinderella" (Lindskoog, *Meeting*, 14). Like the story book character, he felt it was suffering from undeserved neglect. And yet, he told Kathryn, it was in his opinion a "far better book" than *The Screwtape Letters*, whose popularity surprised him.

Today, more than fifty years after that conversation, *The Screwtape Letters* has become a classic; translated into many languages and one of the most well-known works by Lewis. But Cinderella still labors in obscurity, eclipsed by her more popular sister and still waiting for her fairy godmother to appear. And yet these two "daughters" of Lewis arrived only a few years apart, both first appeared in weekly installments, and even in the same Anglican newspaper. Why has one become the favored child and the other not?

Let's begin with *The Screwtape Letters*. The novelty of the approach, skillful writing, and much good advice have given this correspondence wide appeal. Readers willingly suspend their disbelief and enjoy pretending to overhear what devils write to each other. Their humorous names, scarcely-concealed dislike for each other, and the many problems they have with the human race have given hope to millions of readers. Fallen angels may be more powerful than any human, but with God's help and knowing the secrets Screwtape meant to conceal, Hell's deceptions can be avoided and temptations overcome.

Lewis paid a heavy price for his success. His technique ("diabolical ventriloquism" SOT: 152) was a brilliant idea, but it also produced in him "...a spiritual cramp. The work into which I had to project myself while I spoke through Screwtape was all dust, grit, thirst, and itch. Every trace of beauty, freshness, and geniality had to be excluded" (SL: xiv). His personal life was also impacted by the readers who found their lives encouraged and strengthened by the lessons they learned from Screwtape's letters. Many of them regarded Lewis as their spiritual mentor, and hundreds wrote to him. Lewis felt obliged to respond to each; he could (and did) reach many through this ministry, but it cost him many valuable hours until his death.

On the other hand, *The Great Divorce*, as Lewis himself noted, slumbers in relative obscurity. The vivid imagery and dramatic conversations together make *The Great Divorce* a remarkable *tour de force* of the imagination in service of theology. But because that theology arrives through his tour guide, through the dialogues between the Spirits and the Ghosts, by means of many historical figures and literary references, and is even embedded within the landscapes of Hell and Heaven, sorting out all these aspects can be a formidable challenge. The frequent allusions to the Bible and other (often obscure) sources also require an educational background many readers do not have nowadays. I believe this book will help sort things out.

To assist the reader who is not familiar with *The Great Divorce*, or does not have a copy handy, I have provided in Part I a narrative that summarizes the experiences of Lewis throughout his journey. These brief descriptions are given in italicized font for easy recognition.

INTRODUCTION

THE DREAM

The Great Divorce consists of a wealth of details and descriptions built upon a very simple plot. Lewis imagines, as if in a dream, that he finds himself in a rather seedy part of a town that is empty and seems to stretch on endlessly. He finally comes to a bus stop and there joins a small group of people waiting to board. When the bus arrives, most of them find a seat and the journey begins; others have already quarreled and left the bus stop.

The bus soon leaves the ground, flying for hours through an empty void. Lewis meets several passengers during the trip and learns from them more about the grey town that now lies behind and below them. The bus finally approaches land and the passengers disembark to find themselves in a beautiful countryside that ought to be enjoyable and yet is not, since everything is incredibly hard, sharp, solid and dense. Before long, the permanent residents (Spirits) of this place approach, and the passengers (Ghosts) are met by someone they once knew in their earthly lives, or, in one case at least, by an angel. The conversations are gentle (most of the time) but also direct confrontations that are meant to help the Ghosts recognize their sins and ask for Heaven's help in removing them. Each Spirit is ready to assist a Ghost make spiritual progress but few souls are willing to surrender their pride, hatred or unbelief. Nearly all choose to return to the bus for the ride back to the grey town.

An unexpected surprise comes to Lewis in the midst of these experiences; he is hailed by an aged Spirit whose face is both simple and wise. On earth he was George MacDonald,* and Lewis is thrilled to have as his tour guide the Scottish minister who so profoundly influenced him throughout his life, even during his pre-Christian days. Now Lewis has someone to ask about the meaning of his dream, and through his guide, he can both ask and answer his own theological questions. Above all, he learns that the purpose of the journey is not to answer his questions about time, eternity or even to reveal what Heaven and Hell are really like, but to watch human souls determine their own destiny by the choices they make.

The dream comes to a dramatic climax in three parts. Lewis watches breathlessly the final encounter between a husband and wife and describes how Heaven truly blesses those who yield to God. Next Lewis has a vision in his dream of gigantic figures watching pieces move about on a chess board. These represent immortal human souls as they live out their earthly lives. And finally from the east come the first rays of dawn. All nature begins to celebrate, the resurrection is about to… well, Lewis never sees what follows because he is still only a Ghost and the full glory of God is far too much for him to endure. He cries out in terror, the dream is over, and Lewis awakes to find himself on the floor of his office.

THE GENRE OF THE DREAM

One of the reasons Lewis remains so popular with a great number of readers is that he used a wide variety of genres to express himself. Those who like children's stories will find them among the works of Lewis, while those who prefer poetry, correspondence, articles or books will find these also. In brief, Lewis carefully weighed both what he wanted to write, and the literary form that would most effectively convey his thoughts to the readers he wished to reach. *The Great Divorce* well illustrates this harmony between content and form.

The genre of *The Great Divorce* is an open question, because the book has so many unique features. Booksellers classify it as fiction, but many kinds of books are "fiction," so that label is not very helpful. Dante gave his journey to the Spirit World the title of "Comedy," a word that today's reader would interpret as a humorous story. But in Dante's time, a comedy was a sympathetic treatment of the lower classes of society and a plot describing their escape from difficult situations (Parker: 28). Dante gave that genre a transcendent quality by taking his readers to spiritual places not on the earth, and Lewis followed his example.

Today, "comedy" has a very different meaning for us, so I won't use this term to describe Lewis' *Divorce*. Journeys into the spirit world are much closer to the genre known as "apocalypse"; the Book of Daniel and the Revelation of John are two examples of apocalyptic literature in the Bible. In essence, apocalyptic literature is revelatory literature, because the author claims to have received supernatural information about places in the spirit world and/or the future of the world. Typically these revelations come in the form of dreams and/or visions, and there is always a "mediator" (usually an angel) who explains the meaning of the revelations to the human recipient.

Some apocalypses, including the book of Revelation, also feature a Heavenly "tour," wherein the human is taken up into the spirit world and there sees many wonderful (and sometimes frightening) things. The human is led around by a "tour guide"; again, usually an angel, who can answer his questions about the meaning of what he sees. Neither Dante nor Lewis claimed to have experienced an actual trip, but both had their tour guides who "revealed" (so to speak) to them biblical truths concerning God's redemptive purposes and human responses to them.

SOURCES THAT INFLUENCED LEWIS

THE REFRIGERIUM*

Walter Hooper documents that Lewis read the works of Jeremy Taylor* in 1931. In his sermon on "Christ's Advent to Judgement," Taylor quotes from Prudentius, a fourth century Christian poet who wrote about times of refreshment (Latin "refrigerium") in Hell. The basic idea which fascinated Lewis and provided the initial impetus for *The Great Divorce* is "holidays" in Hell, when the fires cool down somewhat, the torments lessen, and the damned are able to relax for a time. (Hooper, CSL: 279)

This interesting tradition plays only a minor role, if any, when Lewis describes his journey to the grey town. He never refers to holidays in Hell, and since his description of the place does not include the traditional fires and torments, there is no place in the dream for them to subside temporarily. Lewis' nod to Prudentius consists of souls being able to leave the grey town, journey to Heaven, give the Spirits a piece of their mind, and then return to Hell. If they choose to return, at least they have had a brief respite from the depressing atmosphere of the grey town. But it's hardly a holiday since Heaven proves to be even more uncomfortable than the grey town.

WILLIAM BLAKE*

Lewis openly reveals his indebtedness to a number of other sources as he writes. In fact, the first word of the Preface to *The Great Divorce* is "Blake". He was referring to William Blake (1757-1827), who wrote *The Marriage of Heaven and Hell*, a satire of Emanuel Swedenborg* whose teachings of morality actually crippled man's energy and genius in Blake's opinion. Lewis is not sure he even understands Blake's *Marriage*, and after reading it more than once myself, I cast my vote with Lewis.

But Lewis had no intention of discussing Blake's views; the title was the starting point Lewis wanted, and Blake represented for him all those who have attempted to blur the distinction between Heaven and Hell. No such "marriage" or even close proximity is possible; Heaven and Hell can never meet, argues Lewis. "If we insist on keeping Hell (or even earth) we shall not see Heaven: if we accept Heaven we shall not be able to retain even the smallest and most intimate souvenirs of Hell" (10).

This insistence upon an absolute "either or" is one of the core principles of the book. Lewis describes a variety of people from all walks of life who have one thing in common; they each must choose between Heaven and Hell. Each of them has a different sin that must be removed, but they, and all of humanity, choose between the same two destinations. No one has been or ever will be exempt from that all-important decision.

Naturally, some have already made many moral choices during their earthly lives, and perhaps those choices have so shaped them that no further choice is possible. Only God knows when all hope is gone. Others, perhaps most humans, are still choosing, and Lewis is particularly interested in souls that have not yet made their final decision. Heaven is a very difficult choice for them because life on earth, a fallen planet, tends to shape souls so that they become reluctant to surrender completely by owning up to faults that have become embedded in their personalities. But if the eternal destiny of a soul is still undecided, Lewis believed that Heaven would lend its assistance to anyone willing to confess his sins and accept the divine grace needed to remove them.

VIRGIL

Lewis is by no means the first writer to envision a trip to the realm of the dead. The great Latin poet Virgil also described such a visit in his *Aeneid*, an unfinished work of twelve books. The first six books of the epic are the Latin counterpart to Homer's *The Odyssey*, and the final six books constitute Virgil's version of Homer's *Iliad*. The epic tells how the Trojan hero Aeneas escapes from the sacking of Troy and makes his way to Italy. During the voyage, a storm drives him to the coast of Carthage, where the queen Dido welcomes him, and under the influence of the gods falls deeply in love with him.

Jupiter recalls Aeneas to his duty, however, and he slips away from Carthage, leaving Dido to commit suicide, heart-broken and cursing Aeneas. But the gods must be obeyed. On reaching Cumae, in Italy, Aeneas consults the Cumaean Sibyl, who tells him his future holds "grim wars" with much bloodshed, and urges him to face them with courage.

Aeneas tells her why he has come; he wishes to visit Anchises his father in the underworld. The Sibyl tells him the preparations he will need to make, and he sets out to complete them. After he has found a golden bough from a tree in the forest to bring to Proserpine, and after they have sacrificed many animals to the gods of Hades, Aeneas descends with her into the realm of the dead. Virgil describes this remarkable tour in Book VI of the *Aeneid*, lines 262-898. The journey is not for the faint-hearted; Aeneas sees "Centaurs and double-shaped Scyllas, and the hundredfold Briareus, and the beast of Lerna, hissing horribly... Gorgons and Harpies, and the shape of the three-bodied shade" (*Aeneid*, Book VI. 285-290).

Aeneas also sees the boatman, Charon, ferry across the river Styx those shades whose bones were buried, while those without a funeral and proper burial must do penance for 100 years before they can cross over to the various places of the dead. He finds Dido, the queen who killed herself when he left her to continue his journey and tries to make peace with her, but she spurns him. Moving on, he hears within a mighty stronghold the agonies of those who did evil on earth, and sees many other places in the underworld. Finally he comes to the Elysian fields, where the souls of the good and brave abide; spending their time relaxing, exercising, reciting poems, singing, and enjoying other pleasant pursuits.

Here in the Paradise of Elysium Aeneas meets Anchises and they embrace. With his father as guide, Aeneas beholds the vast multitude of souls that will once again be born up on earth when their purification is complete. Among them are those who will be his own descendants and he watches in wonder as the future heroes and founders of Rome pass before him. Finally, Anchises escorts him to the two gates of Sleep, and there dismisses Aeneas and the Sibyl. Their journey through the underworld is safely concluded, and Aeneas returns to the ships and still more dangers that await him on his quest to settle in Italy and so fulfill the prophecies that foretold the rise of the Roman Empire.

DANTE

Some twelve hundred years after Virgil described the regions of the dead, Dante Alighieri (1265-1321) decided to visit there as well, but now from a Christian perspective. The great Italian poet paid tribute to Virgil by enlisting him as his guide through the Purgatory and Inferno (Hell) parts of his *Commedia*, later called *La Divina Commedia*, or *The Divine Comedy*, perhaps the last great piece of literature from the Middle Ages. Dante blended together Catholic theology, Aristotelian philosophy, geography, and his own great insights into human nature into a magnificent epic written to call the corrupt Italian society around him to righteousness.

As Dante was influenced by Virgil, Lewis followed in the footsteps of Dante, though he wrote in prose rather than poetry. Dante influenced Lewis in too many ways to list here, so I'll just mention two of the more important nods to Dante. Both writers make their journey after the descent of Christ and both agree that Christ is the only one who was able to conquer Hades. Now those souls who submit to be purified by Christ are able to leave and his conquest also makes possible the visits of Dante and Lewis. Lewis also, like Dante, selected someone he greatly respected as his tour guide: George MacDonald.

But Lewis went his own way in many respects, just as Dante was not limited by Virgil. Dante devoted an entire volume to Purgatory, while Lewis visited only two places. Purgatory seems to be missing, and Lewis used the word only once in his dream (67). Why? Lewis certainly had no theological problem with the concept, as his writings attest. But now his emphasis is upon humanity's two final destinations. And though his dream takes the reader only to Hell and Heaven, in a sense he also visits Purgatory. Those who choose to stay in Heaven will be cleansed of all sins, and any cleansing that occurs after death serves for Lewis the function of Purgatory.

Lewis also broke with Dante by depicting Hell as an urban slum, with fire and brimstone nowhere to be found. And in a very modern touch, those who wish to visit Heaven make the journey on a bus. Dante's souls leave Purgatory only after many years of penitential suffering, while Lewis in more than one conversation between souls and Spirits makes the removal of sin almost immediate. Just confess, let Heaven do its work, and the transformation will begin at once. (In his defense, Lewis wants to focus on the decision of the souls, not the lengthy process of sanctification.) Finally, Dante was a participant in spiritual matters; even reaching through repeated purifications (and only with the help of Beatrice*), the highest circle of Heaven where he enjoyed a vision of God himself. Lewis, on the other hand, remains only an observer throughout his journey. He is there to observe and learn, and never gets any farther than the outskirts of Heaven.

After trying several translations of Dante, the text and notes from Dorothy L. Sayers seemed both clear and strong to me, though admittedly I am not an expert in such matters. So I was much encouraged to find that Lewis shared my opinion of her work. When the third volume of the correspondence of Lewis became available through the heroic efforts of Walter Hooper, it contained several letters Lewis wrote to Sayers expressing his appreciation of her work. After reading her *Purgatorio*, he wrote: "I am really *delighted* with it. Your *Inferno* was good, but this is even better. One wd. say the same to Dante about the originals, no doubt; but then he set the pace, and who would have dared to hope that you could rise with him? ... By gum, it makes one hungry for your *Paradiso* (CLIII, "To Dorothy L. Sayers," July 31, 1955; 634.) And so I will use the Sayers translation for quotations of Dante in this book.

George MacDonald

When Lewis meets MacDonald, he doesn't at first recognize him, then gushes all over him, saying his *Phantastes** was to him as the first sight of Beatrice had been for Dante. Lewis repeatedly acknowledges and praises him in his correspondence and other writings. His influence is well expressed in Lewis' introduction to an anthology for MacDonald: "I have never concealed the fact that I regarded him as my master; indeed I fancy I have never written a book in which I did not quote from him" (*George MacDonald: An Anthology*: xxxii). And so, as Virgil was guided by the Sibyl, and Dante in turn by Virgil (and Beatrice), Lewis continues the tradition and enlists the services of the one to whom he owed so much.

MacDonald proves to be a capable guide, helping Lewis understand what he is seeing and hearing, and answering his many questions. He is also a spiritual mentor, guiding and rebuking Lewis as needed. Even at their first meeting, after modestly deflecting the praise Lewis is showering upon him, he remarks "your memory misleads you in one or two particulars" (65), and turns the conversation from himself to the Ghosts. Lewis begins to ask how they are able to leave the grey town, and receives another mild rebuke for his efforts. MacDonald tells him the *Refrigerium* contains the answer, and observes "A man with your advantages might have read of it in Prudentius, not to mention Jeremy Taylor" (66). Lewis is, of course, familiar with these sources, but has now taken the place of the uninformed inquirer.

The verbal slaps continue throughout the book in this delightful role playing. When Lewis asks if Heaven is a state of mind, MacDonald tells him to "Hush" and cautions him against blasphemy (68). Another warning comes when Lewis belittles the error of a Ghost. Mistaking the means for the end, MacDonald cautions, is a danger "nearer to such as you than ye think" (71). And when MacDonald explains the dangers of the natural affections, Lewis is concerned about being attacked by others should he "dare repeat this on earth." But his guide brushes aside any concerns about his reputation, commenting with a twinkle in his eye "It might do you no harm if they did" (95), and adding that Lewis is not yet "a good enough man" to minister to a mother who has lost a child.

Most importantly, through MacDonald Lewis is free to explain his beliefs about time, eternity, and the ultimate condition and destiny of humanity. Through him, Lewis gives the answers he has, and at the same time establishes the limits of his theology, implying that the reader should do the same. In this world, existence is both defined and limited by space and time, and so we must be content to "see in a mirror dimly" (1 Cor 13:12). But Lewis is quite clear about the choices every person makes and that is why he wrote about his imaginary journey.

THE BIBLE

In addition to all these sources, and others that are listed in Appendix III, by far the most significant was the Bible. This fact about Lewis can not be emphasized strongly enough. Any understanding of Lewis' theological works depends foremost on a thorough knowledge of the Scriptures. To be sure, Lewis was not a "professional" theologian. His formal schooling at Oxford was first in Philosophy, and then he turned to English Literature. But as a theologian myself, I can attest to the fact that his brilliant mind and knowledge of Greek, coupled with his faithful study of the entire Bible, resulted in a very extensive mastery of Biblical imagery and theology. In other words, he was interested in what the Bible said (especially the words of Jesus), the way words were used in the Bible, and the implications of Biblical truth.

Lewis also read the Bible as the inspired, and therefore authoritative, Word of God. The spiritual benefits were more important to him than the intellectual knowledge of the Scriptures. He daily read and reflected upon the Bible, and his writings testify in no uncertain terms that the Bible became the lens through which he viewed and judged his world. The Bible helped him understand the value (and the errors) of ancient mythologies and cultures, the problems of his own times, and even the future of the world as he reflected on the return of Christ.

Readers who are familiar with the theological works of Lewis might find my emphasis upon the importance of the Scriptures for Lewis somewhat questionable. This is because those readers have noticed that Lewis goes "beyond" the Bible in his imaginative works; Biblical truth and theological speculation are blended together. For example, the Bible speaks about angels and sins, but doesn't rank them from lowest to highest as later theologians did. Lewis knew what was Biblical and what belonged to later church traditions, but in a fictional setting, he freely combined them when those church traditions were in agreement with the Scriptures.

And so, more than the Ghosts who described the grey town to Lewis and more even than MacDonald himself, the Bible is the actual "tour guide" that gave Lewis the answers to his questions. The words of Jesus established for Lewis the "great divorce" between Heaven and Hell even while they promise Heaven to every human who chooses to go there. The doctrines and even the language of the Bible, it would be fair to say, underlie every conversation and every landscape Lewis described. To assist the reader, I have listed these Biblical quotations, references, allusions and images in Appendix II near the end of this book.

LEWIS AT WORK

While Lewis had theological and apologetic reasons for undertaking an imaginary tour of places in the spirit world, a variety of other motives as well, including personal reasons, leave their traces in the book. Some scenes simply reflect his fun-loving personality. Many biographers have described him as a "man's man" who enjoyed masculine companionship, jokes that could be a bit risqué, and hearty laughter. If nothing else, Lewis demonstrates a light touch even when treating a subject as serious as a person's eternal destiny; the same quality that helped make *The Screwtape Letters* so readable. Lewis' claim that he has forgotten his glasses—as if souls needed glasses—so he won't have to read the poet's work, or the quarrel that erupts with guns and knives but harms no one since the participants are already dead: such scenes evoke a smile or chuckle.

A more solemn prerogative comes to Lewis by virtue of his journey; the "populating" of Hell. Dante showed little reluctance in consigning various popes and many other important people of his time to appropriate punishments he believed they earned by neglecting the church and meddling in affairs of the state and various corruptions, but Lewis is far more reserved with his choices. He rounds up a few of the usual suspects (Julius Caesar*, Genghis Khan*, Napoleon*, etc.) from the past, but only two contemporaries, whom he disguised under a pseudonym or no name at all. Most of his attention goes to fictitious characters who each struggle with one particular sin he wishes to warn against. All things considered, he takes little pleasure in naming the inhabitants of Hell. If retribution were his goal, we would be better acquainted with some of his schoolmasters and fellow students. Salvation, not condemnation, is what Lewis wants to see, and the same is true of the Spirits who have come a long way from the heights of Heaven for the solemn business of persuading people to choose Heaven.

This "solemn business" (the stakes are eternal, after all) naturally caused Lewis to do some soul-searching. Glimpses of Lewis himself appear in some of the characters, and damned ones at that, as he reflects upon how his life might have gone. The poet echoes the early ambition of Lewis to be a published (and famous) poet. The Episcopal Ghost rejected "crude salvationism" to gain a wider audience and Lewis also met the same temptation. Sir Archibald fell into the trap of substituting the means for the end; and Lewis shows through the warning of MacDonald that people such as himself are particularly susceptible to this subtle snare. And it's worth noting that Sir Archibald's downfall was Spiritualism, and that Lewis himself came under the sway of this strangely attractive belief system. More than ten years would pass until he would return to the faith he had as a child.

The characters Lewis chose to describe have convinced me that *The Great Divorce* is more autobiographical than any other of his fictional writings since *The Pilgrim's Regress*. In essence, through several of them Lewis is giving thanks to the One who got him "on the bus" of salvation. He is saying, in effect, "There, but for the grace of God, go I." Lewis elsewhere testifies to the influence of his soul-searching upon his writing. He disagreed with those who judged that the insights of *The Screwtape Letters* were the product of years of theological study. "They forgot that there is an equally reliable, though less creditable, way of learning how temptation works. "My heart"—I need no other's—"showeth me the wickedness of the ungodly" (SL: xiii).

The Structure of This Book

Part One: The "Sociology" of The Great Divorce

To manage best the complexity of the book, I have divided the discussion into three parts. Since the main focus of Lewis is upon people and the choices they make, people—that is, their souls—will be the starting point. I shall call the first part of the discussion the "Sociology" section since the focus here will be upon the souls Lewis meets, the Spirits (sanctified souls) that meet them, and the decisions the souls make.

Lewis chose to emphasize regular people like those he met in life; people with little or no theology, others with many beliefs, and even people bruised by life and angry with God. Lewis is open to the possibility of any of these people choosing Heaven after they die, and we might wonder why anyone would pass up the opportunity. But Lewis thinks many will and the reasons become clear as he watches them make their choices in his dream.

Lewis encounters souls in four different spiritual conditions. The first and most lost are those who have chosen to move so far from the bus stop they will never make the journey. Next are those who do embark on the remarkable journey from the grey town to the edge of Heaven, but decide to make it a round trip. Another trip may be possible, but Lewis seems to imply that the decision to go back "down" is final. Lewis refers to all of the souls in the first two groups as "Ghosts."

The third group consists of those who decide to leave the grey town for good and make their way into Heaven. Only one soul actually chooses to stay, but "group" is still appropriate since many other souls have already yielded to God before the story begins. The one soul who decides to remain in Heaven is changed from a Ghost to a Spirit while Lewis watches. Finally, there are the souls who come down from the heights of Heaven to invite the Ghosts to stay and accompany them into deeper Heaven. They once were Ghosts themselves, but Lewis refers to the souls in the fourth group as "Spirits" to indicate they have been cleansed of sins and are now at home in their new "environment." The pagination of GD seems to vary with each new edition, so in this section, my chapters will follow those of the book. Most of the chapters of GD are quite brief, so the reader can easily follow the discussion no matter which edition is being used.

PART TWO: THE "GEOGRAPHY" OF THE GREAT DIVORCE

After we have made the acquaintance of the people Lewis observed, the discussion will return to the beginning of the book to study the places he visited. Lewis described these places in the spirit world as if they were places on earth, since (as he knew full well) humans have no other vocabulary at their disposal. But since Lewis never had an actual "tour" of the spirit world, do his imaginings have any value? In the opinion of this author, they have great value. Not because Lewis revealed how Hell or Heaven actually looks, sounds and feels, but because he created his landscapes to convey theological truths, as I will demonstrate.

Three landscapes are described in this journey. Lewis first found himself in a dreary slum that seemed to go on forever. Its tremendous size, its emptiness, the climate and even the time of day all work together to convey what Lewis wanted to say about that part of the spirit world. Then he got on a bus and rode (flew, actually) across a vast abyss that separated the slum from his destination. Finally, he (and the other passengers) disembarked into a beautiful setting even larger than the slum. Part II will be the "Geography" section of this book, with a chapter each for the grey town, the Abyss and Heaven.

PART THREE: THE THEOLOGY OF THE GREAT DIVORCE

After I have explained the theological implications of the choices people make and the places Lewis described, it will be time to join together the rest of the pieces of Lewis' theology in this book. More specifically, the central discussion will include how Lewis understood the descent of Christ into Hades, what he accomplished there, the implications of his descent for all humanity, and the parts both humans and Heaven play in the process of sanctification. Even the bus itself, "heraldically coloured," and the Bus Driver* who seemed "full of light," have their theological meanings in the dream. All of these subjects, and others, are spokes radiating outward from the central issue; the final and most important choice every human must make.

Lewis clearly believed Christ descended into Hades, and that sanctification continues after death, but what precisely were his views, and can they be supported by the Scriptures? Does his theology imply the doctrine of Purgatory, and if so, does Lewis agree with the Catholic understanding of Purgatory or does he have his own views? Do people really get a "second chance," and if so, would that remove the urgency of the Great Commission? And even if the Church does someday carry out the instructions of Jesus so that everyone alive hears about the good news of salvation in Christ, what of the untold billions who didn't hear because they happened to live before Christ or before the Gospel came to their cultures? Will they be lost or will God somehow reach them as well? Much of this discussion will reflect my earlier treatment of sanctification after death in *C. S. Lewis: A Guide to His Theology*, and I am grateful to Blackwell Publishing Ltd. for their generous permission to use material from this book.

Lewis faced these and similar questions with all the Scriptures, imagination and logic at his disposal. He was honest enough to acknowledge the limits of his understanding, even while he arrived at conclusions so far-reaching they pertain to every son of Adam and every daughter of Eve who have ever lived and ever will live. Read on, and I think you will agree with me that *The Great Divorce* may be the most important theological book Lewis ever wrote.

Part I

The "Sociology" of *The Great Divorce*

Multitudes, multitudes, in the valley of decision! (Joel 3:14)

Chapter 1:

At the Bus Stop

THE OFFENDED WOMAN

Lewis dreams that he has been walking for hours through a dingy, deserted town that seems to stretch on forever. Rain is falling and an unchanging dusk adds to the gloomy setting. He finally notices a small group of people waiting at a bus stop. Hungry for some human companionship, he joins the queue, wondering if there will be room on the bus for everyone.

No sooner does Lewis get in line, but a "waspish" woman leaves, remarking to the man (perhaps her husband) next to her, "Very well, then. I won't go at all. So there." Then the man departs as well, protesting that he had only been trying to please her (14).

The first impression Lewis gives of the people in the grey town is their tendency to quarrel with each other. Indeed, their inability to get along is the chief characteristic of the place. One wonders, even on earth are there any marriages immune from the "wounded pride" syndrome? (And not just marriages are affected.)

Lewis touched on this subject in *The Screwtape Letters*. Screwtape explains this as unselfishness gone bad and tells Wormwood to strive for this result:

> In discussing any joint action, it becomes obligatory that A should argue in favour of B's supposed wishes and against his own, while B does the opposite. It is often impossible to find out either party's real wishes; with luck, they end by doing something that neither wants, while each feels a glow of self-righteousness and harbours a secret claim to preferential treatment for the unselfishness shown and a secret grudge against the other for the ease with which the sacrifice has been accepted (SL: 122).

What led to this falling out between the woman and the man? Lewis doesn't reveal their prior conversation, but the man does say "Pray don't imagine that I care about going in the least. I have only been trying to please *you*, for peace sake" (14). His words imply that he is willing to sacrifice his own desires to please her, a noble act which will earn him the "glow of self-righteousness" that Screwtape was advocating. She in turn would rather be the martyr than let him sacrifice for her and gain moral superiority over her. Neither is happy, they both feel justified in nursing a secret grudge against the other, they miss the bus, and Screwtape scores another victory.

THE SHORT MAN AND THE BIG MAN

The quarreling couple leaves and Lewis moves up in the line. But this brings him next to a Short Man who is scowling at him with obvious disapproval. Before long, a Big Man comes to his rescue.

We aren't told what the Short Man dislikes about Lewis; only that he tells the man in line before him that he is not used to this "sort of society". (14) But the Big Man takes Lewis's side, and seems to think the Short Man was referring to both of them. When Lewis doesn't respond to the insult, the Big Man acts, striking the Short Man in the face and knocking him into the gutter. "Let him lay" he says in his own defense, "I'm a plain man... and I got to have my rights same as anyone else, see?" (14) Just where his "rights" come in isn't clear, unless the Big Man thinks he has the "right" to dispense his version of justice wherever needed. But there is no doubt about how the life he led on earth has shaped his soul. He is a bully who insists on his own "rights" and will use force to preserve them. He has replaced the Golden Rule with rule by might.

THE UNISEX COUPLE

The line continues to shrink when another couple steps away. They are so unisex in dress, voice and mannerisms that Lewis is not sure of the gender of either one. More interested in each other than catching the bus, they leave—perhaps to a secret rendezvous somewhere (15). There is, of course, nothing wrong with being in love. But spiritual matters should have the highest priority.

THE CHEATED WOMAN

Just before the bus arrives, the line shrinks again when a man offers a woman who is concerned about there not being enough seats on the bus five bob to exchange places with him. (A "bob" is a shilling; in 1945 five shillings would be worth approximately ten dollars today.) He takes her money, but then refuses to give her his place when she leaves her own. The others laugh and refuse to let her back in line.

The bus arrives, painted in vivid colors, and operated by a figure of imposing authority. The passengers complain to each other about his radiant appearance; one even wants to strike him. Nevertheless, they do embark, fighting "like hens" (15) to get on, and yet the bus is only half full after everyone has taken a seat. Lewis enters the bus last, and takes a seat in the back hoping to avoid the others, but to no avail.

THE POET

No sooner is Lewis seated than a "tousle-headed youth" joins him, eager to talk to someone. He seems to identify with Lewis, as did the Big Man, and expects him to share his feeling of superiority to the others. Things are now reversed. The Short Man in the line didn't like the company of Lewis, while this youth prefers it to the other passengers. Either way, Screwtape would be proud. He reassures Wormwood in his third letter that even though his patient has started attending church, all is not lost since he thinks "he is showing great humility... in going to church with these... commonplace neighbours" (14).

Few themes carry so much personal meaning to Lewis as this tendency of people to choose favorites, or enemies; often simply on appearance. His recollections of his time at Wyvern College were chiefly focused on the misery caused by all the cliques. The younger boys were abused by the older, including sexually, and Lewis would later write "I believe that in all men's lives at certain periods, and in many men's lives at all periods between infancy and extreme old age, one of the most dominant elements is the desire to be inside the local Ring and the terror of being left outside" ("The Inner Ring" in WG: 146). He adds in the same essay, "Of all passions the passion for the Inner Ring is most skillful in making a man who is not yet a very bad man do very bad things" (154). No wonder Screwtape reminded his nephew that for his patient, "The idea of belonging to an inner ring, of being in a secret, is very sweet to him" (SL: 113).

The young ghost next tells Lewis he can't understand why the passengers on the bus want to come at all, since they have become used to the cinemas and shops of the grey town and now find life there comfortable. He claims that he missed the first bus because he was trying to "wake people up." But, as it turns out, his intention was not to send them to the bus stop but to start a "little circle" of people who would listen to what he had written and give him intelligent feedback. Now the unfortunate Lewis is cornered, and the would-be author pulls out a sheaf of papers hoping that he will look at them.

For all his faults, the young ghost functions as the first "tour guide" for Lewis. His complaints about the lack of intellectual life in the grey town help Lewis understand the flavor of the place. To his credit, he still has some interest in the life of the mind, though he is mistaken in his belief that the intellectual pursuits he can provide will help reform the grey town. Just then, the bus begins its journey and Lewis is spared the role of poetry critic.

A Reader's Guide to The Great Divorce

CHAPTER 2

On the Bus

THE POET'S STORY

As soon as the bus begins to move it leaves the ground and climbs higher and higher over the grey town. As far as the eye can see, the rooftops reach to the horizon.

Before a violent quarrel on the bus rescues Lewis from this would-be "literary giant," he learns that the young man regards himself as a poet who has been singularly "ill-used" in life (18). None of the five schools he attended recognized his capabilities, appreciated his unique talents or provided examinations that were fair to him. Once he received a university education, he came to understand that his schooling had been biased because capitalism "vulgarized" the intellect, with the result that his genius did not receive due recognition (18).

Next came the war and when Russia joined forces with capitalist countries he had no choice but to become a conscientious objector. This was not a popular status, and so he decided to move to America, until that country also joined the war. Seeking a just society, he wanted to settle in Sweden but funds were lacking. The allowance from his Victorian father was grossly inadequate, and his girl friend proved to be possessive and a "mass of ... monogamic instincts" (she wanted to marry him and thought he should be faithful to her) and tight with her money. Only one option was left to him; suicide. Even then, he was sent to the wrong place.

Oh, the poor man – so mistreated! But beyond his self-centeredness, what is really interesting about the Poet ghost is that Lewis could easily be describing himself. The specific details about the Poet's life reveal Lewis' special interest in this person. And there are many points of correspondence. His father, Victorian in outlook and standards, meant well, but communication between the two was difficult and often strained after the death of Lewis' mother. He also was sent to five schools: Wynyard School or "Belsen" for two years, 1908-1910; one term at Campbell College from September to

December 1910; then Cherbourg House from 1911-1913 (called Chartres in SBJ); Malvern College (called Wyvern College in SBJ) from 1913-1914, and finally Oxford University, beginning in April 1917. He returned to his studies in January 1919 after military service and finished in 1923. (I'm not including his private tutelage under Kirkpatrick from 1914-1917 since he was the only student, he was not at a school with other students, and his studies there were much to his liking.)

Like the poet, Lewis didn't "fit" into any of these schools, though in all fairness, their influence upon him was often for the good. He disliked the emphasis upon sports, the cliques that excluded others, and the mistreatment of the younger boys by the older. He also suffered under at least one cruel (later certified as insane) headmaster, and many of his interests were outside of the prescribed studies.

His great youthful passion was to be a poet. There were obstacles, to be sure. Exams at Oxford required mathematics, Lewis's worst subject, and he was spared failure only because he was exempted from that (unfair!) part of the tests because he had served in the military. His father's allowance was inadequate, though in all fairness to him, Lewis did not tell him that he was supporting Mrs. Moore* and her daughter when he returned to his studies at Oxford after military service. And when Lewis wrote about the educational system in the west, he agreed (through Screwtape) with the Poet on the bus that the brightest students were being squelched because "democracy" was now interpreted (thanks to the philological experts of Hell) to mean that no student should excel over the others, lest the others be traumatized (SPT: 161-165).

The Poet ended his own life; did Lewis ever contemplate suicide? There is not much evidence either way, but his diary does reveal that his programs at Oxford were so fatiguing that at times death seemed more inviting than continuing with his studies. (AMR, 8 Sept 1923: 265) And just like the Poet, Lewis was at the center of the Inklings for many years; a small literary group that read portions of poetry or books in progress to each other. But by then the drive for fame had given way to the desire to place God above his own reputation, and to mentor the many people who wrote to him for spiritual advice.

And so Lewis has told part of his personal story through the Poet ghost; but only a part, thanks to the grace of God. Perhaps the Poet ghost will indeed stay, as he assured Lewis. But since he is looking forward to a place where his "finely critical spirit" will at last find "Recognition" and "Appreciation" (19), the environment of Paradise will not be to his liking until he makes the story of Lewis his own.

C. S. Lewis Goes to Heaven

Ikey's Plan

Before the Poet can inflict his poetry on Lewis, a quarrel breaks out. Knives are drawn, pistols are fired ("Make my day! Make my day!"), but since everyone is already dead, no harm is done. When the dust clears, Lewis finds himself in a different seat, next to an "intelligent-looking man with a rather bulbous nose and a bowler hat" (20).

Ikey is Lewis' new companion and he also serves as a tour guide, telling Lewis even more than the Poet did about the people in the grey town. The place is so empty, he explains, because people are constantly quarreling with each other. Unable to get along, they simply move away from everyone else. Those who have been there the longest are now light years away from the bus stop and there is no chance they will ever get on the bus.

But Ikey has a solution. The way he sees things, the problem is not just the quarrels people have with each other. After all, that's only human nature. Life back on earth was just the same. No, the real problem is that the souls in the grey town have no genuine needs. People can get whatever they want just by imagining it. And so Ikey has gotten on the bus so that he can bring back something real from Heaven. That way, with something to buy, people will start coming together again. He'll turn a profit and benefit society at the same time. Lewis wonders out loud if this economic reform will result in fewer quarrels, and Ikey isn't sure about that. Anyway, if he can bring people together, it may be possible to form a police force to keep order.

Lewis has certainly asked the right question, and he knows from experience what the answer will be. Communism at first certainly seemed promising from an economic standpoint, asking "from each according to his ability" and promising "to each according to his need," but history has shown that the system doesn't work. The industrious person loses the incentive to produce, since the state will take most of it and distribute it to others who are less motivated. And why should people be motivated since the state will provide for them even if they are poor workers?

Ikey means well, but economic systems exist to manage the production of goods and services. They can't magically transform people into model citizens willing to sacrifice for others. And the state that controls the distribution of goods and services all too often becomes corrupted by so much power. Economic reforms can certainly improve the living standards of a nation, but they do not bring salvation of souls. If they did, wealthy societies would have little need for police and prisons. The only hope for the earth, not to mention Purgatory, is the transformation of the soul that only God can accomplish. Until then, quarrels will continue to produce ill-will and separation.

NAPOLEON AND OTHERS

Through Ikey, Lewis learns the names of several historical people who now live a great distance from the bus stop. Tamberlaine* is there, a Mongol conqueror with a reputation for cruelty, and Genghis Khan another Mongol ruler of the same repute. Much earlier than either of these is Julius Caesar, the first dictator of Rome, and then forward again in time to Henry the Fifth* (21).

The last member of the "old chaps" is Napoleon. Since he lived fairly recently compared to the others, his house (huge and built, logically enough, in the Empire style) can still be seen from the bus stop, though only as a tiny pin-prick of light. Since his arrival, he has gone downhill. Unable to stop pacing back and forth, he blames his defeats upon Josephine*, the English, and his generals Soult* and Ney*. Ikey is able to provide Lewis with this description of Napoleon because he spoke to two people who went to see him; a trip that required fifteen thousand years.

Napoleon is the only one of this group that Lewis actually describes (the others are too far away, so to speak), and the constant pacing of the French emperor reveals that he is no longer able to change and accept responsibility for his plight. He is truly in Hell. Dante leads the way here; all those in his Hell never rest. Their activities reflect their sins, and are "without rhyme or reason, which alternate only with a meaningless monotony or a sterile fixity. In all it does and is, damnation is without direction and purpose. Why not? It has nothing to do and all eternity to do it in" (*Purgatory*: 61).

THE EPISCOPAL GHOST

When Ikey tells Lewis that dusk in the grey town will become night, a fat, clean-shaven man in the seat in front of Lewis turns around to refute Ikey's belief. And so Lewis discovers that one of the passengers is a theologian. In fact, back on earth he was a bishop in the Episcopalian Church. The old theology of Hell and judgment are only outdated superstitions in the bishop's opinion, and Lewis learns from him that dawn will soon come, not night, symbolizing the grey town inhabitants turning toward spirituality. Not immediately, of course, but the bishop insists that change, that dawn, will come, adding a literary quotation to support his hope:

> And not through "Eastern windows"* only,
> When daylight comes, comes in the light.

Furthermore, now that the souls in Purgatory are freed from their bodies and the world of matter, the Episcopal Ghost believes the grey town is actually a spiritual city in which humanity can begin fully to realize its creative potential. In his opinion, Ikey's materialism will take humanity in the wrong direction. Spirituality, not economic reform, will release the "creative functions" of mankind.

Lewis used Ikey and the bishop to represent the two most important paths toward the reformation of human society that have been repeatedly tried throughout history. Ikey represents all those who have attempted to address the evils of society through economic reform. The twentieth century saw two major expressions of reform through economics (and revolution, if necessary), and both were reactions against ecclesiastical corruption. First, Communism appeared, doing away with the Russian tsar, characterizing religion as "the opiate of the masses," and promising to help people here and now. Later, in Latin America and Africa, Liberation Theology also called for economic reform, again rejecting any version of religion that promised Heaven to its followers but gave them little or no help in this life.

On the other hand, the theology of the Episcopal Ghost has its roots in ancient Gnosticism, which held that matter is evil and spirit good. The path toward spirituality is denial of the body and many in the early church turned to asceticism under the influence of Gnostic thought. Some even lived in caves or perched on top of pillars for many years in their struggle for purity. Now that the souls in the grey town have finally escaped their bodily "prisons," they are free from the sinful desires of the body and spiritual progress will no longer be held back by the struggle between body and soul.

Gnosticism became so strong an alternate version of Christianity emerged, teaching that Christ could not truly have been God in the flesh, since God as pure Spirit would not contaminate himself with matter. Rather, the man Jesus became divine when the Spirit came upon him at his baptism. Later, the Spirit departed during the crucifixion, leaving the man Jesus to die on the cross. In the recently discovered Gospel of Judas, a very Gnostic document, Judas did Jesus a favor by betraying him. The betrayal led to his death and death brought freedom from his body, the prison of flesh that Jesus needed to escape.

Both approaches have their strengths. Economic reforms do improve the lot of people, and the appetites of the body do need controlling. But escaping poverty through economic reform will not change the sinful nature of mankind. And the sins of the soul have a greater potential for evil than those of the body. Nor did Christ teach that the material universe is evil. Mankind must exercise stewardship over the earth, not reject it; use the physical body for His glory, not renounce or abuse it. The body will, after all, share in God's redemption through the resurrection. In the end, mankind's only hope is the inner transformation that comes through the divine life the believer has through Christ.

Lewis now rides for hours in silence as the bus floats in a "pure vacancy" (26). The light grows stronger and the air sweeter, but the other passengers object when Lewis attempts to lower a window to let in some fresh air. "Want us all to catch our death of cold?" Finally the bus ascends to the top of a cliff and glides to a stop. Fighting and cursing, the passengers exit the bus until only Lewis is left.

"WE SEEMED TO BE FLOATING IN A PURE VACANCY...
NO LANDS... NO STARS... ONLY THE RADIANT ABYSS."

CHAPTER 3

Arriving at Heaven

You have come to Mount Zion... and to the spirits
of just men made perfect. (Heb 12:22-23)

Where human spirits purge themselves,
and train to leap up into joy celestial.
(*Purgatory*, Canto i. line 506: 73)

FIRST IMPRESSIONS

Lewis is the last one off the bus and when he steps outside, he finds himself in a space so huge that the solar system is an "indoor affair" by comparison (28). The pastoral landscape is beautiful in appearance, but everything is so solid and heavy that the blades of grass are as sharp and hard as diamonds. Even a single leaf is too heavy for Lewis to lift. In stark contrast to the landscape, the ghosts appear as transparent bubbles; mere stains on the countryside. One of the passengers is overcome by such real surroundings and darts back into the bus. And for the first and only time the bus driver speaks, telling the Big Man (who only wants his "rights") that everyone may stay there as long as they wish (29).

A RESPECTABLE GHOST

One of the more respectable ghosts interrupts Lewis's contemplation of the new world around him, and wonders if the management of the place has made a mistake in allowing the ghosts to come here, since they find their surroundings so uncomfortable. He soon drifts away, displeased to find himself in the company of his inferiors, and expecting someone to meet him. Lewis does not see his fate, but how will he respond when he meets others so superior to himself?

Alone once more, Lewis scans the distant horizon and sees forests, hills and valleys. Still farther away, mountains loom so high their tops are lost to sight. Hours later, bright objects appear and as they come closer, he can see that they are people; very solid, ageless in appearance, some robed and others not, but all of them glorious in appearance. Two more ghosts run for the bus in terror at the sight of them. Even Lewis becomes uneasy, and huddles together with the other passengers.

CHAPTER 4

The Big Man and Len

As the solid people arrive, they move with purpose toward the ghosts and Lewis minds his manners by moving away so as not to overhear. But the Big Man follows him, and in turn a spirit follows the Big Man, so Lewis has no choice but to follow the conversation.

The Big Man recognizes the spirit who has come to meet him as Len and is amazed to find him in Heaven, since back on earth Len had murdered Jack, a mutual acquaintance. Len readily acknowledges his crime: "Of course I did. It is all right now" (33); in fact Jack is there too and the Big Man will soon meet him.

But the Big Man cannot accept the fact that things are "all right now" and that Len admits such a serious crime so easily. Len is a "bloody murderer," (but now redeemed by blood) and the Big Man is outraged to find him enjoying life in Heaven while he was down on earth living as best as he could in a place "like a pigstye" (33).

Forget about things being "all right," it's high time Heaven gave him his *rights*, insists the Big Man. That's not a good idea, Len cautions him, because you really weren't all that good and God has something better than what you (really) deserve. In fact, you were a cruel boss and you made things difficult for all of your employees, your wife and your children. Len confesses his hatred of him back on earth, adding that he murdered him many times in his heart. "That is why I have been sent to you now; to ask your forgiveness and to be your servant as long as you need one" (35-36).

Len does his best to persuade the Big Man to acknowledge his faults, but he wants no part of a Heaven that allows murderers to become citizens of Heaven. As for himself, admitting his faults and asking for grace would be too demeaning. "I'm not asking for anybody's bleeding charity." Len replies (with a wonderful pun), "Then do. At once. Ask for the Bleeding Charity" (35). But

Len's invitation means giving up entering Heaven by his own efforts, and, just as bad, relying on Len (a murderer, after all) to help him get there. Encouraged by his ability to resist both Heaven's charity and Len's "apron strings" (36), the Ghost returns to the bus, grumbling and whimpering along the way.

CHAPTER 5

The Episcopal Ghost and Dick

Lewis is alone once again, but not for long. Two lions appear and begin playing together. He moves away to find the river he had seen before, hoping it will be a safer environment. Once there, he overhears another conversation; this time, between a blindingly white Spirit named Dick and the Episcopal Ghost who told Lewis on the bus that the grey town was a spiritual city and that morning would soon arrive. (from Chapter 4 on, Lewis capitalized "Spirit" and "Ghost")

The clerical Ghost cheerfully greets Dick, expecting that his theological views will have mellowed since their discussions back on earth when he seemed rather narrow in his theology. But Dick hasn't changed, and says that the Ghost has been in Hell, sent there for being an apostate. The Ghost takes offense at this, surprised that people would be punished for honest opinions. The soul-searching begins as Dick reminds him...

> You know that you and I were playing with loaded dice. We didn't want the *other* to be true. We were afraid of crude salvationism, afraid of a breach with the spirit of the age, afraid of ridicule, afraid (above all) of real spiritual fears and hopes... Having allowed oneself to drift, unresisting, unpraying, accepting every half-conscious solicitation from our desires, we reached a point where we no longer believed the Faith (41-42).

Lewis tasted many philosophies, including atheism, and no doubt "crude salvationism" struck him as distasteful before he finally gave in to God. He and the clerical Ghost trod the same path for a time. But now, to his credit, he plainly tells the Ghost (and so the readers of his book) through the Spirit named Dick to "repent and believe" (43). There is no other way but crude salvationism, and it begins with repentance, followed by accepting the "Bleeding Charity" the Big Man Ghost found so offensive. Why "Bleeding"? Because crude salvationism means trusting in the blood (death) of Christ for the forgiveness of sins and forsaking all the modern attempts to remove from Christianity the primitive concept of atonement by blood.

Repentance, of course, means sincere regret for the sins of one's past, but Lewis takes a healthy approach to this difficult chore: ask forgiveness and move on. He almost makes it seem easy as the Spirit counsels the Episcopal Ghost: "I have been talking of the past (your past and mine) only in order that you may turn from it forever. One wrench and the tooth will be out. You can begin as if nothing had ever gone wrong" (42).

The yanking of a tooth metaphor would later become one of Lewis' preferred ways of describing Purgatory.

> My favourite image on this matter comes from the dentist's chair. I hope that when the tooth of life is drawn and I am "coming round," a voice will say, "Rinse your mouth out with this." *This* will be Purgatory. The rinsing may take longer than I can now imagine. The taste of *this* may be more fiery and astringent than my present sensibility could endure. But More and Fisher shall not persuade me that it will be disgusting and unhallowed. (LTM: 109)

This view is certainly more encouraging than years and years of penitential suffering. But speculations of what Purgatory might be like should not obscure what is more important; Lewis' healthy approach to repentance. "We should, I believe, distrust states of mind which turn our attention upon ourselves. Even at our sins we should look no longer than is necessary to know and to repent them: and our virtues or progress (if any) are certainly a dangerous object of contemplation" (CLIII, "To Walter Hooper," November 30, 1954; 535).

Evidently, Dante helped Lewis on this point.

> We must beware of the Past, mustn't we? I mean that any fixing of the mind on old evils beyond what is absolutely necessary for repenting our own sins and forgiving those of others is certainly useless and usually bad for us. Notice in Dante that the lost souls are entirely concerned with their past. Not so the saved (CLIII, "To Mary Willis Shelburne," June 5, 1961; 1274).

The Ghost still maintains that he "believes," despite the fact that he has abandoned the central doctrines of the faith, so Dick tries to make things easier by asking if the Ghost can at least believe in him, knowing that if they set off together toward the mountains, full faith will eventually be attained. The Ghost finally seems willing to consider this, but on one condition: a guarantee that he will be able to utilize his talents in "an atmosphere of free inquiry" (43). No, replies Dick, "you are not needed there," and besides, Heaven is a place of answers, not inquiry.

The Episcopal Ghost cannot accept this version of Heaven; such finality would be stagnation. In his opinion, "to travel hopefully is better than to arrive" (44). To counter this mistaken opinion, the Spirit repeatedly describes the wonders of "arriving;" of finding God himself. "You are in sight of Heaven" (43), "I will bring you to the land not of questions but of answers" (43), "Your thirst will be quenched" (44), "I will bring you to the Eternal Fact, the Father of all other facthood" (45), and the greatest of all promises, "You shall see the face of God" (43. To see God is also known as the Beatific Vision*). Sadly, none of these seem to outweigh the attraction of traveling hopefully, even with no destination in sight.

A little more probing by Dick uncovers just how liberal the Ghost's theology has become. He no longer views God as a Real Person but as an abstract concept, a "Supreme Value." The Ghost describes Him as "purely spiritual. The spirit of sweetness and light and tolerance—and, er, service" (45). Other essential Christian doctrines have suffered the same fate.

In that spirit of service to others, the Episcopal Ghost suddenly remembers that he can't accompany Dick into Heaven; he has a paper to read next Friday for the theological society down there. His topic will explore how the theology of Jesus would likely have been more tolerant had he lived longer. What a waste; Jesus never had the chance to become more mellow with age. And the crucifixion was not the atonement for the sins of the world but a "disaster". The conversation, and with it, all hope for the Episcopal Ghost, comes to an end. Unperturbed, and full of plans for his Theological Society, the Ghost departs while singing "City* of God, how broad and far" (47).

Lewis devoted more space to this sad encounter than any other conversation between a Ghost and a Spirit save one (Sarah Smith* and Frank; Chapters 12-13). The importance of the Ghost is that he represents liberal theologians who find "crude salvationism" offensive and barbaric in an age of tolerance "Whatever works for you" is a much more enlightened perspective on life. What used to be regarded as sin is now simply an "alternate lifestyle." "Spirituality" is the thing now, and Christianity does not have a monopoly on that. Besides, hasn't the modern Church left behind more the primitive concept of gods who demand blood sacrifices? And so the bishop found the path to popularity when he replaced the gospel of salvation with the social gospel: service to others.

Yes, service to humanity has been (and should be) one of the strengths of Christianity and Jesus Himself set an example of service when He washed the feet of His disciples. Service to others is the way many people first begin to grasp the love God has for them, but service is not salvation. Those who are served may become more receptive to the message of salvation, but all the deeds of loving kindness cannot bring forgiveness of sins and new life. Forgiveness comes from God, and that new life must also come from above. "This is the whole of Christianity. There is nothing else… the Church exists for nothing else but to draw men into Christ, to make them little Christs"

(MC: 155).

This Ghost was the sort of minister Screwtape recommended to Wormwood, when he discovered (with displeasure) that his patient was still attending only one church. He advises Wormwood to get his patient into the habit of trying a variety of churches in order to find one he likes, and to help Wormwood get started, he has already done some research on two churches nearest the patient. In the first is a vicar "who has been so long engaged in watering down the faith to make it easier for a supposedly incredulous and hardheaded congregation that it is now he who shocks his parishioners with his belief, not vice versa" (SL: 73-74).

The Episcopal Ghost not only "watered down" the faith, he also fell into an intellectual trap when he lost sight of the fact that the point of a journey is to reach the right destination. This danger of forgetting the destination is not restricted to the field of theology, but since the goal of theology is to point men to God, theology is the map of the most important journey of all. There is undeniable pleasure in the search for truth, but what is the point of the journey, Lewis asks, if there is no hope of arriving at the truth? Paul warned Timothy that there would come a time when people would be constantly learning but never able to arrive at a knowledge of the truth (2 Tim 4:7). The bishop and those like him are a fulfillment of that prediction.

The Episcopal Ghost is certainly an optimist; I'll give him that. He recognizes a "certain confusion of mind," "regrettable jealousies," and tempers out of control (46) in those who attend his Theological Society, but feels confident that reform will eventually come as he reads his papers. But theology, Lewis insists, rightly understood, is not the destination, but the roadmap to Christ who is the destination. Since the Ghost has rejected that destination (indeed, any destination) and reduced God Himself to a vague "spirit of service," his "theology" will benefit no one. As Screwtape reminds Wormwood, "Men or nations who think they can revive the Faith in order to make a good society might just as well think they can use the stairs of Heaven as a short cut to the nearest chemist's shop" (SL: 109).

Since the optimistic Ghost believes that people in the grey town will become more enlightened in their theological views over time, as he himself did, he regards the place as a spiritual city. In fact, he regards it as Heaven, in a sense, full of potential for "indefinite progress" (whatever that means). He actually intends, thanks to his liberal theology, to "marry" Heaven and Hell and this misconception is precisely what Lewis is attempting to prevent.

CHAPTER 6

Ikey, the Golden Apple and the Waterfall

After the Episcopal Ghost leaves, Lewis decides to avoid the painful grass by walking on the river. He falls once but then he gets the hang of it and begins to make progress. After an hour or so, the water becomes rougher and he moves to the bank of the river to take advantage of the large, smooth stones in that area. He soon comes to a waterfall so huge and loud his senses on earth would not have been able to take it all in. Near the waterfall is a tree with "golden apples*."

While admiring the beautiful apples, something catches the attention of Lewis and he turns to see what appears to be a hawthorn bush acting strangely. On closer inspection, Lewis discovers that the movement is not the bush but Ikey next to the bush, and he is trying to approach the tree with golden apples. But he has discovered as did Lewis that going anywhere in the sharp grass and iron-stiff flowers is difficult and painful. A gust of wind dislodges several apples, and Ikey now has within his reach the "something real" he spoke to Lewis about back on the bus. He tries to gather several of them, but they are so heavy he is forced to settle for the smallest. Lewis is amazed that he actually manages to lift it, though the exertion is agonizing. Bent over double, Ikey sets out, inch by inch, on his torturous *via dolorosa** back toward the bus and disappears from sight (51-52).

Ikey, to his credit, has chosen well, and likely intends to make many trips. But who will buy such apples? The fruit of divine life and the reality it brings will not be welcome in the grey town where self-deception reigns supreme. Heaven cannot come down into Hell; not even a single apple. Each person must choose to leave the grey town, if choice is still possible, and once Heaven has transformed the soul, such apples may be freely enjoyed. Ikey means well, but he is going in the wrong direction. Even when the Spirit of the waterfall tells him that there is no room in the grey town for the apple, he persists in his attempt to bring Heaven down to Hell through economic reform (51).

CHAPTER 7

The Cynical Ghost

After Ikey leaves, Lewis begins to feel uncomfortable in the presence of the waterfall that seems to have a life of its own. Fatigue sets in, and he heads back downstream, wishing he could refresh himself by taking a dip.

Hearing a voice, Lewis turns to see a stranger leaning against a tree. He's a tall, lanky "hard-bitten" Ghost; the kind of person that gives Lewis the impression of being reliable. He is well-traveled, but his experiences have convinced him that behind the scenes, a "World Combine" is running the show and that tourist places all over the world are simply advertising gimmicks that don't deliver what they promise (54).

Even Heaven and Hell are run by the same secret group, he tells Lewis, and things are no better than they were on earth. More gimmicks. No interesting people are "sizzling on grids" in Hell, and Heaven is also a disappointment. You can't eat the fruit or drink the water, walking on the grass is like walking on knives, and if it rains, the drops will go right through you like bullets. When Lewis wonders if Heaven and Hell are actually at war with each other and not under the same management, the Hard-bitten Ghost points out that if the inhabitants of Heaven really did want to get rid of Hell and rescue the souls there, they could have done so long ago. "But obviously the last thing they want is to end their so-called 'war'. The whole game depends on keeping it going" (56).

Since neither place seems suitable for human habitation, Lewis asks the Ghost what course of action he would take if he had the chance. But once again, he blames the management rather than doing some soul-searching. If they are so smart they can run the show, why don't they build something their publics will enjoy?

> All this poppycock about growing harder so that the grass doesn't hurt our feet, now! There's an example. What would you say if you went to a hotel where the eggs were all bad; and when you complained to the Boss, instead of apologizing and changing his dairy-man, he just told you that if you tried you'd get to like bad eggs in time (56)?

The Hard-Bitten Ghost belongs to the Conspiracy branch of humanity that has been around for a long time and attracts large numbers of adherents even today. They suspect that the world is controlled by a powerful group working behind the scenes; perhaps the Jews, or the Opus Dei. The Freemasons have had their turn, as have the Knights Templar and the World Bankers. The Ghost failed to control his suspicions (a little honest research would have cleared things up) and he became so cynical that he lost the capacity to believe anyone; even God. As Lewis noted in his correspondence: "A belief that one has been misused, a tendency ever after to snap and snarl at 'the system'— that, I think, makes a man always a bore, usually an ass, sometimes a villain" (CLIII, "To Laurence Harwood," August 2, 1953; 353).

Under that cynicism lies a deeply rooted self-centeredness. Heaven will have to change to agree with him, not vice versa. Nor is he interested in helping things along. Let the "management" fix things up; it's their job, not his. Still further down, under the cynicism and self-centeredness, this Ghost uses the inductive approach to form his "theology." He visited many places in his travel around the world and sensed that large corporations and powerful people had built them. And this is true. But he let his experiences and his cynicism form his concept of God, rather than beginning with the character of God as revealed in the Bible. Since Heaven can't change to suit his demands, the Hard-Bitten Ghost will never stay in the painful environment of Heaven.

CHAPTER 8

The Self-Conscious Ghost and the Unicorns*

Lewis parts ways with the cynical Ghost feeling uneasy and discouraged. "Horrid myths and doctrines"(58) came to mind; perhaps the cynical Ghost had good reason to be suspicious. Heaven now seemed to him not only uncomfortable but downright dangerous.

Under the spell of his negative encounter, Lewis recalls how the gods had punished Tantalus* after he had stolen the food and drink of the gods and brought them down to mortals. Even Christian tradition brought no comfort; the saints were said to behold the "smoke of Hell"* that rises forever and offers no escape. Then he thought of William Cowper*, the poet and hymn writer who suffered from deep depression and attempted suicide several times. Cowper had devoted himself to Christ but still could not escape the terror of damnation. And Lewis had seen lions earlier; what if they returned? Even the insects darting about were so solid in that place they would go right through him if one should fly into his face. What if it rained, or if he had gotten too close to the spray from the waterfall? If only he could find proof that a Ghost could stay there...

Not yet willing to return to the bus, Lewis moves on and soon comes to a clearing. There he sees a Ghost trying to conceal herself in some bushes. She had once been stylishly dressed by earth standards, but now seems shabby and naked in the pre-morning light of Heaven. Soon a Spirit approaches and offers to lead her back in the right direction, toward the mountains. But she is consumed by the shame of being transparent in the company of such solid people. "I'd never have come at all if I'd known you were all going to be dressed like that," she tells the Spirit (60). The Spirit urges her to face up to her shame. "If you will accept it - if you will drink the cup to the bottom - you will find it very nourishing" (61). For a moment, she nearly makes the attempt, but then draws back. The Spirit has no choice but to try something drastic; he blows a horn and a herd of unicorns appears, the smallest of them twenty-seven hands high. They are full of spirit, prancing and snorting and tearing up the turf. The

Ghost screams and begins to run away but Lewis does not see the outcome for he also is terrified and flees for his own safety.

This is an important scene for Lewis, and he meant much more by it than just the clothing of a woman who once was a "fashion plate." The latest styles once concealed her nakedness on earth, but now in Heaven "... no creature is hidden, but all are naked and laid bare to the eyes of the one to whom we must render an account (Hebrews 4:13). When any human is confronted by the Divine presence, the awareness of sin will produce shame and the desire to retreat, to go anywhere to just escape that scrutiny. But shame is good, Lewis holds; without it, who will feel the need to repent? To seek divine help?

> ...Unless Christianity is wholly false, the perception of ourselves which we have in moments of shame must be the only true one... A recovery of the old sense of sin is essential to Christianity. Christ takes it for granted that men are bad. Until we really feel this assumption of His to be true, though we are part of the world He came to save, we are not part of the audience to whom His words are addressed. We lack the first condition for understanding what He is talking about (PP: 57).

Lewis later learns from his tour guide that the purpose of the frightening encounter with the unicorns was to get the woman's mind off herself long enough for her to overcome her shame and accompany the Spirit into Heaven. The unicorns are at least seven feet high at the "withers" (the cusp of their neck) so they would certainly be intimidating. Some might find this scene rather far-fetched, but the message is what matters: Heaven will, in love, find a way, if any exists, to reach a troubled soul.

CHAPTER 9

Lewis Meets His Tour Guide

"Canst thou be Virgil? thou that fount of splendour
   Whence poured so wide a stream of lordly speech?"
   Said I, and bowed my awe-struck head in wonder;

Thou art my master, and my author thou,
   From thee alone I learned the singing strain,
   The noble style, that does me honour now.
                          (*Hell*, Canto i. 79-81; 85-87: 73)

Things are not going well for Lewis. Paradise is beautiful, to be sure, but everything is solid and dense, and most of it is hard and sharp as well. And his conversation with the Hard-bitten Ghost has left him discouraged and vividly aware of the dangers around him. Sure enough, the very next encounter with a Ghost sends him flying in terror from the unicorns. His flight brings him to open country, but in which direction should he go? He doesn't fit in, dangers surround him, and yet who would want to return to the dismal place he left behind? Just in time, things take a turn for the better.

A voice asks "Where are ye going?" and Lewis turns to see another of the Solid People sitting on a rock. For the first time, he directly looks at a Spirit. Two images seem blended together in that face; he is at once an ageless Spirit shining with glory, and yet an "old weather-beaten man who might have been a shepherd" (64). He is, in fact, George MacDonald, the person to whom Lewis owed so much.

Lewis joyfully acknowledges his debt to MacDonald with high praise, comparing the impact his writings had upon him, even before his conversion, with the influence of Beatrice who made such a powerful impression upon Dante for his spiritual good. In Dante's journey through Hell, Purgatory and Heaven, Virgil is his guide at first, but he was a pagan on earth and so cannot lead him into Heaven. Only the Christian Beatrice can accomplish that. And as she does so, she serves not only as his guide, but also becomes, as in life, the means God uses to sanctify him until he can even gaze at God himself in the highest Heaven.

In like fashion, Lewis is also helped by several Ghosts who can explain life in the grey town. The Poet tells him about the shops and cinemas there, and Ikey explains why the souls are so far apart, but neither of them is able

"My name is George. George MacDonald."

to understand why Heaven and Hell are so far apart. That honor goes to MacDonald, whose deep insights into spiritual matters helped the earthly Lewis toward Heaven.

Questions for MacDonald pour out of Lewis once he learns his identity, but he learns that the answers will not become clear until he is beyond space and time. The reason he has been given this dream is so that he can study the choices people make. Those who make the wrong choices justify themselves in many ways ("I served my country right or wrong, I sacrificed everything for my Art, I didn't let anyone deceive me" 68), but there is always a common thread: "something they prefer to joy—that is, to reality" (69). In the end, MacDonald explains, quoting Milton, the choice of every lost soul is: "Better to reign in Hell than serve in Heaven" (69, *Paradise Lost*, Book 1). Pride may seem trivial in a sulking child, but if not mastered, MacDonald warns, the child may grow up to become prideful adults like Achilles* and Coriolanus* who turned on their own people when circumstances went against them.

MacDonald's warning about pride, as the greatest sin of all, causes Lewis to wonder if any will be lost due to "mere sensuality." This may sound strange to the modern reader, with society's fascination with affairs (sometimes videotaped and somehow appearing on the internet), marital unfaithfulness, revealing fashions, eating disorders, and the like. In fact, the careers of many celebrities seem to benefit when such indiscretions are made public.

Surely these shocking sins are among the worst. Why else would society be so preoccupied with them? But Lewis reveals a very different perspective on sin as he reflects upon his body in one of his letters.

> I have a feeling for the old rattle-trap. Through it God showed me that whole side of His beauty which is embodied in colour, sound, smell and size. No doubt it has often led me astray: but not half so often, I suspect, as my soul has led *it* astray. For the spiritual evils which we share with the devils (pride, spite) are far worse that what we share with the beasts: and sensuality really arises more from the imagination than from the appetites; which, if left merely to their own animal strength, and not elaborated by our imagination, would be fairly easily managed. (LAL: 108; Nov 26, 1962)

A common misconception among Christians is that our struggles with sin will end with death, since we will finally be free of the body with its appetites. Not so, Lewis reminds us. Angels don't have bodies like ours, and yet some of them have fallen due to sin. The soul continues on after the body dies, and must be cleansed. As for the "undignified vices," as Lewis terms them (69), they certainly are sinful when abused, but the body has its limits. One can only eat so much, engage in sex so often, stay awake so long, and so forth. But what are the limits of greed, hatred, envy or pride? Note that Dante places lustful souls on the seventh and highest cornice of Purgatory, just below the earthly Paradise. Prideful souls, on the other hand, are properly much lower down toward Hell, on the first cornice.

With a renewed sense of purpose and security, Lewis gladly accepts the guidance of his new tour guide, and they set out to explore the spirit world so that Lewis can observe various souls as they struggle with the greatest choice of all. As he guided Lewis during his life journey on earth, MacDonald will be a faithful interpreter until the dream is over.

SIR ARCHIBALD*

In the course of their first conversation, MacDonald describes someone who embodied the human tendency to hold on to a pleasure even after it has become clear that true joy will never be found through that pleasure.

MacDonald informs Lewis that a certain "Sir Archibald" recently arrived on the bus but didn't stay. It seems that his earthly life was consumed by a desire to discover if there truly is survival after death. This obsession led him to mediums, trances, and all sorts of psychical investigations which took him to many exotic places and cost great sums of money. Finally, he died, came to the grey town, and eagerly rode the bus to Heaven. But only disappointment met him there; everyone had already survived. "His occupation was clean gone. Of course if he would only have admitted that he'd mistaken the means for the end and had a good laugh at himself he could have begun all over again like a little child and entered into joy. But he would not do that. He cared nothing about joy. In the end he went away" (71).

At first glance, this Ghost seems to be based upon a "tragic, Irish parson" Lewis came to know when he returned to his studies at Oxford after his military service. No longer a believer, his single obsession was "human survival;" and yet he was not interested in seeing God, nor improving his soul to make it fit for immortality, or even meeting dead friends. "All he wanted was the assurance that something he could call "himself" would, on almost any terms, last longer than his bodily life" (SBJ: 202).

But a closer look at the biographical details Lewis provides of "Sir Archibald" reveals so many specific, historical facts that he must be describing someone else. Sir Archibald's obsession with the afterlife and his activities during the historical era in which Lewis places him point only to one individual: Sir Arthur, not Sir Archibald. Namely, Sir Arthur Conan Doyle. The famous creator of Sherlock Holmes lived from 1859 to July 7, 1930, making him roughly a contemporary of Lewis and this may be the reason he disguised his identity. Or perhaps Lewis simply did not wish to be inundated by thousands of letters from fans outraged that he had "sent" the creator of the world's most famous and beloved detective to Hell.

Sir Arthur Conan Doyle set out to be a doctor, but success in the medical profession eluded him. On the other hand, his Sherlock Holmes stories were doing very well and so he abandoned his (non-existent) practice to devote himself to his detective (and Dr. Watson) at 22B Baker Street. His stories brought him fame and fortune, but he became more and more interested in the afterlife when he unsuccessfully tried to keep his wife alive after she contracted tuberculosis. Eventually, his interest in Spiritualism and his membership in the Society for Psychical Research began to crowd out his writing. His quest for information about the spirit world took him to many countries, including America, Australia and Africa, where he was not always well-received, as noted by MacDonald. The biographers state that he spent over 250,000 pounds on his obsession; a considerable sum in those days. Based on the value of the British pound sterling in 1900, the amount Holmes spent on psychic research would be equivalent to approximately thirty million dollars in purchasing power today.

"How fantastic!" Lewis responds after hearing MacDonald's description of Sir Archibald. "Do ye think so?" MacDonald replies. "It is nearer to such as you than ye think" (71). Nowadays, "fantastic" often means "great" or "really cool," but Lewis is using one of the older and more proper meanings of the word: "foolish" or "irrational." Paraphrasing, Lewis is saying "I can't believe anyone would get so caught up in a quest that he would refuse Heaven." This earns him a rebuke from MacDonald: "It's not so hard to believe; in fact, people just like you are particularly susceptible."

The tendency to substitute the means for the ends, MacDonald continues, "is the subtlest of all the snares" and "nearer to such as you than ye think" (71). Lewis (through MacDonald) then gives four examples from his own times that demonstrate how easy it is to lose sight of the goal: those who set out to prove the existence of God (apologetics) but in time no longer care about God himself, those who spread Christianity but give no thought to Christ, those who collect valuable books but no longer treasure their contents, and those who organize charities but lose their compassion for the poor.

The warning Lewis aimed at himself through MacDonald's is a signal that Lewis knew he also had the tendency to replace the ends with the means. And in fact, Lewis and Doyle walked the same road, a fascination with Spiritualism, for more than a few years. Only with considerable difficulty; indeed, one could say only by the grace of God, did Lewis escape its hold on him, and even then, never completely.

Lewis himself provides the details in his autobiography. Miss C. (identified by Hooper as Miss G. E. Cowie, CLI: 20), the Matron at Cherbourg House, the school Lewis began attending at the age of thirteen, was herself looking for the answers to life. The search took her into such belief systems as Theosophy, Rosicrucianism, and Spiritualism. Lewis fell under her spell: "there might be real marvels all about us, the visible world might be only a curtain to conceal huge realms uncharted by my very simple theology" (SBJ: 60).

After Lewis became a Christian, his fascination with the occult took on new significance. Just as Doyle succumbed to the lure of Spiritualism, Lewis later realized he had been drawn toward the same "Turkish Delight" (addicting passion) of the soul by the example of Miss Cowie, and not for his good.

> ...That started in me something with which, on and off, I have had plenty of trouble since—the desire for the preternatural, simply as such, the passion for the Occult. Not everyone has this disease... It is a spiritual lust; and like the lust of the body it has the fatal power of making everything else in the world seem uninteresting while it lasts. It is probably this passion, more even than the desire for power, which makes magicians (SBJ: 60).

Lewis did not blame the matron for this lust, this sickness. "Better say that the Enemy* did this in me, taking occasion from things she innocently said" (SBJ: 60). Lewis barely recovered, and even then the sickness never completely left him ("Off and on, I have had plenty of trouble since"). But Doyle, in the opinion of Lewis, never did escape from the obsession, and its "fatal power of making everything else in the world seem uninteresting" finally made even Heaven itself of no interest to him in Lewis' dream.

When Lewis did recover, and became familiar with the Scriptures, he came to believe that spiritualism

> ...is a sin as well as folly. Necromancy (commerce with the dead) is strictly forbidden in the Old Testament, isn't it? The New frowns on any excessive and irregular interest even in angels. And the whole tradition of Christendom is dead against it. I wd. be shocked at any Christian's being, or consulting, a medium (CLIII, "To Mary Van Deusen," December 14, 1958; 997).

Lewis becomes uncomfortable under MacDonald's piercing gaze and changes the subject. All this talk about letting good causes replace a desire for God himself is hitting too close to home.

Why, Lewis asks his guide, (recalling the Cynical Ghost who maintained that Heaven could have done away with Hell long ago if God really wished to do so) does Heaven not take more aggressive steps to help the Ghosts? But

MacDonald explains that the Spirits have come a great distance already and that going further would achieve nothing. "The sane would do no good if they made themselves mad to help madmen" (72). In other words, the Ghosts are where they have chosen to be, and when that decision is final, not even Heaven can change them.

The Grumbling Ghost

At this point, the "shrill monotonous whine" of a Ghost interrupts the conversation between Lewis and his tour guide. A woman is describing her experiences on earth and in the grey town and the Spirit sent to help her seems unable to interrupt her monologue.

The grumbling Ghost explains to the Spirit how she couldn't get along with others because they were so self-centered and inconsiderate of her needs. The doctor bungled the operation that eventually killed her ("I was murdered, simply murdered:" 73) and sent her to the grey town prematurely. And, to add insults to injury, the nursing home "starved" her and no one came to visit her.

As they move out of hearing, the Spirit still waiting to get a word in, Lewis remarks that she doesn't seem to deserve damnation; she's only a poor old woman who feels neglected and has gotten into the habit of grumbling. There is hope, MacDonald informs him, if she is indeed a grumbler. Heaven will take the necessary steps to reach the woman inside. "If there's one wee spark under all those ashes, we'll blow it till the whole pile is red and clear. But if there's nothing but ashes we'll not go on blowing them in our own eyes forever. They must be swept up" (74).

Lewis goes on to reveal an essential insight into the cumulative effect of moral choices. Nearly everyone can recall times when some perceived injustice or bad set of circumstances led to grumbling. The danger comes when grumbling becomes a habit; a response to every injustice real or perceived. "… there may come a day when you can do that no longer. Then there will be no *you* left to criticise (sic) the mood, nor even to enjoy it, but just the grumble itself going on forever like a machine" (74).

The Flirtatious Ghost

Leaning on MacDonald's arm, Lewis is able to walk faster than before, and the presence of his guide seems to awaken his senses. He begins to enjoy the beauties of the country, and even imagines he's becoming a bit more solid. Soon they encounter other Ghosts; one of the saddest being a woman who was the opposite of the self-conscious woman scared by the unicorns.

This Ghost is contorting her face and twisting her body each time a Spirit attempts to converse with her. Lewis is puzzled by her strange behavior until he finally realizes she is trying to attract the Spirits. She is of course unsuccessful. "If a corpse already liquid with decay had arisen from the coffin, smeared its gums with lipstick, and attempted a flirtation, the result could not have been more appalling" (75). Muttering "Stupid creatures," she returns to the bus.

Old habits die hard. This woman was accustomed to attracting the opposite sex by using her physical qualities, and modern western societies certainly encourage this approach in countless movies and advertisements. Lewis touched upon this theme many times in his writings, warning against the lustful emphasis upon the feminine form that he saw all around him.

Writing to Owen Barfield, he explained that he had come to realize that a woman's desire to be admired explains how Venus is depicted in mythology. "Venus is a female deity, not 'because men invented the mythology' but because she is. The idea of female beauty is the erotic stimulus for women as well as men... a lascivious man thinks about women's bodies, a lascivious woman thinks about her own. *What* a world we live in!" ("To Owen Barfield," June 19, 1930, CLI: 904.)

Later, during WWII, Lewis returned to this theme in *That Hideous Strength*. As Jane is being led by Camilla Denniston through the gardens at St. Anne's, strange thoughts came into her mind.

> Freud said we liked gardens because they were symbols of the female body. But that must be a man's point of view. Presumably gardens meant something different in women's dreams. Or did they? Did men and women both feel interested in the female body and even, though it sounded ridiculous, in almost the same way? A sentence rose in her memory. "The beauty of the female is the root of joy to the female as well as to the male, and it is no accident that the goddess of Love is older and stronger than the god" (THS: 62).

No sooner had she left the garden and entered a room to wait for an interview with Ms. Ironwood than she saw a book lying on a table, opened to these very words. Coming to the next sentence she read: "To desire the desiring of her own beauty is the vanity of Lilith, but to desire the enjoying of her own beauty is the obedience of Eve, and to both it is in the lover that the beloved tastes her own delightfulness" (THS: 63).

Perhaps Lewis here explains the downfall of the Flirtatious Ghost. It's normal for a woman to desire to enter into a permanent relationship with one man who will appreciate and love her for all her qualities, but the insecurity of the Flirtatious Ghost led her to attempt to lure many men into desiring her. When flirting is occasionally successful, it often results in both people leaving their respective spouses. Eventually, left uncured, the poison can spread beyond this life and into eternity.

A Variety of Ghosts

Many other Ghosts now pass before Lewis and his guide. Some want to teach the Spirits about Hell, others have come to tell the Spirits about their own misery, as if suffering somehow made them superior to those who enjoyed the sheltered life of Heaven. All of them, Lewis observes, had no curiosity about the place they were visiting. They came only to talk and "repelled every attempt to teach them" (76). One by one, they returned to the bus when their attempts at "educating" the Spirits failed.

And yet these were not the worst. For many other Ghosts, the desire to describe Hell was only the beginning of a stronger desire: the intention to somehow bring Hell up into Heaven.

Planning Ghosts urged the Spirits to take over Heaven, kill the animals, and smooth out the horrible grass by paving over it with asphalt. Activist Ghosts urged the Spirits to conquer Heaven and offered their assistance. Materialistic Ghosts tried to convince the Spirits that there was no life after death, and still others of monstrous appearance came from a great distance to the bus stop just for the opportunity to tell the Spirits what they really thought of them and their privileged existence.

Lewis even saw the final horror; those who were afraid of themselves because they had become Ghosts. Recalling something he read in Tacitus,* Lewis realized that in the end, the only option left to them was to terrify others to keep from being frightened of themselves. And so these came to Heaven to frighten the Spirits, with predictable results. How can mere stains on the landscape hope to intimidate those who are flowing over with love and joy?

What a picture of despair. The Ghosts seem closed up, full of spite and beyond hope. Yet even for these Lewis leaves the door open a tiny crack. They did take the bus, after all. Some of this sort, MacDonald informs Lewis, do decide to stay. "Those that hate goodness," he explains, "are sometimes nearer than those that know nothing at all about it and think they have it already" (77-78).

Pause

The descriptions of the interactions between Hell and Heaven have now progressed from individual Ghosts, most of whom wished to bring Heaven down to Hell, to groups of Ghosts whose agenda was just the opposite. All attempts in either direction, of course, are doomed to failure. A "great divorce" is the permanent and only reality.

Is Lewis now finished with the Ghost/Spirit interactions? The reader might come to that conclusion, since Lewis is now describing Ghosts in bunches rather than individually, and the conversations between Ghosts and Spirits no longer take place. But what appears to be the final summation of the Ghosts is only a very brief pause, and leads into the final five interactions that will build up to the climax of the sociological part of the book. In the order of presentation Lewis meets the Artist Ghost (the relationship between humanity and nature in the arts), a female Ghost (the marital relationship between a Ghost wife and a Spirit husband), another female Ghost (relationships between parents and children), a Ghost with a red lizard (physical appetites), and Sarah Smith (the marital relationship between a Ghost husband and a Spirit wife).

The Artist Ghost

MacDonald calls the attention of Lewis to a Ghost with a familiar appearance, and soon Lewis realizes he has seen him in the papers; he was a famous artist. The Spirit who meets him was also an artist, and so they begin to talk "shop." Struck by the beauty around him, the Ghost wishes he had thought to bring his supplies with him, but the Spirit tells him he has to change into a "Person" first. To do that, he has to forget about painting because if he is interested in seeing Heaven only to depict it in art, he will never really see it. Nor will he ever develop into full humanity. "To enter Heaven is to become more human than you ever succeeded in being on earth; to enter Hell, is to be banished from humanity" (PP: 125).

With this discouraging news, Heaven begins to lose its appeal to the Artist. His art has brought him fame, and instead of celebrating this success, Heaven tells him he is not yet fit to paint. The reason he will have to relinquish the brush for a while, the Spirit explains, is that when he began his career, he saw glimpses of Heaven in nature. In fact, his ability to help others see those glimpses through his artistry was the reason he became famous (78-9). But as his career advanced, painting itself gradually replaced his desire for Heaven.

The Artist Ghost listens, and then asks when he will be allowed to paint. More bad news. "Never," comes the answer, "if that's what you're thinking about" (79). Heaven, not painting, must be the object of desire, and the Artist must make that his goal once again. "Light was your first love; you loved paint only as a means of telling about light" (79). The Artist recalls his early days, and agrees with his friend, but of course he has matured since then.

Actually, as MacDonald explains, he has fallen into the trap that awaits every poet, musician and artist: being "drawn away from love of the thing he tells, to love of the telling till, down in Deep Hell, they cannot be interested in God at all but only in what they say about Him" (80). With his focus now on self, his art now serves to express his own personality, and his reputation becomes more important than Heaven. The artist must return to his first love of the light, which Lewis here uses as a symbol of God. In Heaven, "The Glory flows into everyone, and back from everyone: like light and mirrors. But the light's the thing" (81).

There is a cure for the Artist's "inflammation;" to drink from a fountain "up there in the mountains… a little like Lethe"* (80). The Spirit promises "when you have drunk of it you forget forever all proprietorship in your own works. You enjoy them just as if they were someone else's: without pride and without modesty" (80). When Heaven has done its work, self will die and be reborn, cleansed from pride, ambition and desire for fame.

Things seem to be going well; the Artist takes the arm of the Spirit for support and they begin their journey to the mountains. But then he expresses a desire to meet Claude Monet* and Paul Cezanne,* famous Postimpressionist and Impressionist artists (81). The Spirit doesn't know if they are there (Lewis hesitates to place them in Hell) since he is newly arrived in Heaven and hasn't met everyone yet. Surely, the Ghost remarks, famous people like Monet and Cezanne would be widely known there. But they aren't famous, the Spirit explains, because in God's sight, everyone is famous. Well then, the Ghost muses, one must be content with one's reputation on earth since it doesn't survive in Heaven.

But their journey toward the mountains is soon cut short. As they converse, the Spirit informs him that they are no longer famous even back on earth, and that no one would pay more than five pounds for their works. "What's that?" asks the Ghost, taking his arm away from the Spirit. "Do you mean those damned (excuse his language) Neo-Regionalists* have won after all?" (81). "Yes," replies the Spirit, laughing at him and at himself, for his earthly reputation means nothing to him now. "We're dead (another wonderful Lewis pun) out of fashion" (82)! But this shock is too much for the Ghost and he returns to the bus, Heaven forgotten, and furiously making plans to restore his good name.

Lewis had a keen appreciation for the fine arts, and his correspondence has hundreds of references to the great literature, music, and other cultural expressions of the western world. But he did not view the enduring expressions of human culture as spiritual accomplishments in and of themselves, but as "a storehouse of the best (sub-Christian) values" ("Christianity and Culture" in CR: 23). They must be put to a spiritual use if they are to glorify God. "The thing to which, on my view, culture must be subordinated, is not (though it includes) moral virtue, but the conscious direction of all will and desire to a transcendental Person in every thought and act" ("Christianity and Culture" in CR: 26).

Could the Artist Ghost be a real person? Lewis has left several clues; more than necessary for a purely fictional character. He was a famous artist back on earth, and evidently possessed true talent for when he has fully entered heaven, "there'll be some things which you'll see better than anyone else" (79). His first love as an artist was light, and when he painted landscapes, he "caught glimpses of Heaven" in them, and so helped others see those glimpses. But then his reputation became more important.

The Artist Ghost wants to see Cezanne and Monet, implying that they may have influenced him to adopt an Impressionist style of painting. In fact, he asks about Monet by his first name (Claude), suggesting that he was on a first-name basis with him. Finally, with Neo-Regionalism in ascendency back on earth, his work is of little value in both Europe and America, revealing that he had been popular on both continents during his life.

That's not much to go on, but if Lewis saw photographs of the now-deceased artist in the papers, he must have died during Lewis' life before he wrote *The Great Divorce*, and after Lewis had reached the age of young adulthood. The Spirit who meets the Artist Ghost was also an artist, preceded the Ghost in death, and must have known him well since he was sent to assist him into Heaven.

These clues do point to a particular artist: John Singer Sargent (1856-1925). Sargent was born to American parents in Florence, Italy, because his mother was a hypochondriac who insisted that Europe was better for her health than America. Even there, the family moved frequently, but to the benefit of Sargent who was able to visit the museums and art galleries of many countries and be educated in Italy, France and Germany.

Sargent's artistic talents surfaced early and his father succeeded in getting him admitted to the studio of Charles-Emile-Auguste Durand, a portrait painter in Paris who used the professional pseudonym Carolus-Duran. There, he was strongly encouraged to study the work of Velazquez, and in the opinion of at least one art critic, he learned much from Velazquez about the importance of light.

> Sargent's first great works—I think, in fact, his greatest works— were done in that mood of darkness splashed and split by light that re-creates the inner force of the Spanish master... One of them, the *Venetian Interior*...has obsessed me...the interior space seems to have a gentle phosphorescence of its own: the mauve and silver halftones give it a certain submarine quality, perhaps referring to the watery essence of the city of canals and lagoon, and the light is seen as through water... Because the spaces have a light that is quiet in comparison with the enveloping light we see through the apertures, they seem enclaves of shadow in a world of radiance (Danto: 51-52).

Other critics concur with Danto's view of this work. One writes: the "distinctive light effect characterizes the exoticism of a particular locality... (Prettejohn: 12). And in reference to Sargent's early work, she adds "the management of light is perhaps the most striking evidence of the young artist's technical aplomb..." (Prettejohn: 16).

Sargent's career moved from one success to another, with one exception. His portrait of Madame Pierre Gautreau (Madame X) shocked Paris since he portrayed her with one shoulder strap hanging down over her arm (how times have changed) and the uproar led Sargent to leave France and "set up as a sort of superficial Impressionist in England. Up to that critical moment he was a child of fortune but a very deep painter indeed, and on the basis of what he achieved in the early 1880's he might have gone on to be very great as well" (Danto: 51). Sargent would call London home for the next thirty-nine years, until his death in 1925.

But his career did flourish; Sargent was eagerly sought after by presidents and captains of industry in America, and his reputation soared. But he finally tired of portrait painting, describing himself as a pimp, and spent the rest of his life in England. "There he turned into a rather superficial artist, the maker of dazzling portraits and dubious Impressionist studies... But all light has fled from these turgid works: one feels, for all the glamour of his career, that he had made a profound mistake" (Danto: 53-54).

Reading Danto's views of Sargent's Impressionist works, one would think Danto and Lewis had been corresponding with each other about them.

> Sargent tried Impressionism, but that is not a country for Old Masters, and I feel he had no internal understanding of what revolutions in touch and vision Impressionism implied. His watercolors have the look of examples of how to do watercolors, and if one did not know them to be by Sargent, one would suppose them resurrected from the annual of some provincial watercolor society... I find his drawings equally dry, for all the certitude of touch and his perfect draftsmanly control. In none of the work after 1884 do we sense any urgency of feeling or the presence of a soul (Danto: 55).

Sargent's Impressionist works have been compared to Seurat and Cezanne, and their influence upon him would explain the desire of the Artist Ghost to meet Cezanne. He did meet Monet in 1876 at an Impressionist exhibition, came to admire him greatly, and painted him several times. Sargent even entered into a business deal with Monet to purchase Manet's *Olympia* for the Louvre, which would account for him (the Artist Ghost) being on a first name basis with Monet.

Lewis obviously shared Danto's estimation of Sargent's career, if indeed Sargent is the artist he portrayed in his dream. The clues Lewis gave do seem to point to him. He remained a superb artist during his life, and Lewis does not fault him for his Impressionist work. But the pursuit of success and popularity through portrait painting (which he indeed enjoyed) came at the expense of his earlier work which showed "the presence of a soul" and such great promise in the mastery of light.

CHAPTER 10

Robert's Wife and Hilda

The next conversation takes place between a female Ghost and a Spirit named Hilda. The subject of discussion is Robert, the Ghost's husband on earth, and Hilda appears to have been Robert's mother. The Ghost reminds Hilda how unselfishly she had sacrificed to make something out of Robert; getting him better friends, pushing him to work harder for promotions, moving into bigger houses, entertaining the right sort of people, and so on. But she only met with resistance and resentment, and in the end, though Robert had a nervous breakdown, at least she had done her duty by him and his collapse surely wasn't her fault.

Now she has come up in the bus because no one down there will pay any attention to her and she needs someone to manage. She doesn't really want to meet Robert, but if Heaven will let her have him again, she'll go the extra mile and once again try to improve him. (Somewhere, no doubt, Robert is pleading not to be sent to her.) Hilda never really has the chance to slow the torrent of words before the Ghost becomes so angry that she suddenly flickers out of existence and disappears (88).

Lewis had interesting views on unselfishness. He characterized women as *taking* trouble for others, while men tried to avoid *giving* trouble to others (SL: 121). But when caring for others gets out of control, when a person needs to be needed, those who receive the care can get smothered by it. Mrs. Fidget, wrote Lewis, lived for her family, who endured for years her controlling ways. "The vicar says Mrs. Fidget is now at rest. Let us hope she is. What's quite certain is that her family are" (FL: 50).

CHAPTER 11

Two Loves Gone Wrong

PAM AND REGINALD

The conversation between a Ghost named Pam (the first Ghost to be named) and a Spirit named Reginald is the third longest and also one of the most painful. Pam expects to meet her son, but her brother comes instead to explain things. To begin with, her son Michael is in Heaven, but he hasn't come to meet her, Reginald explains, because he wouldn't be able to even see his mother in her present condition. She needs to be "thickened up a bit" (90). And that growth in her spirituality will come only when she learns to want someone else beside her son. The Ghost reluctantly agrees, since this will bring her closer to her son, but the Spirit won't accept her motive. "You're treating God only as a means to Michael… the whole thickening treatment consists in learning to want God for His own sake" (90).

We next learn that her "love" for her son was so controlling ("I gave up my whole life…") that God had to call him home prematurely. "It was a case for surgery… there was a chance that in the loneliness, in the silence, something else might begin to grow" (91). But it didn't because she couldn't let go. She kept his room exactly as it had been, and she refused to acknowledge that her husband Dick and their daughter Muriel also grieved for Michael. "It wasn't against Michael they revolted: it was against you—against having their whole life dominated by the tyranny of the past: and not really even Michael's past, but your past" (93).

> As Reginald tries to convince his sister that Michael belongs to God, not her (even though she was his mother), MacDonald steers Lewis away from the conversation. The encounter may continue for quite a while and they have heard enough to understand Pam's obsession.

Lewis is left to wonder about maternal loves for children and husbands and learns from his guide that all natural loves will rise again and live forever in Heaven, but only if they first have been buried. Otherwise, to make a natural love into a god actually allows it to become a demon. "The higher and mightier it is in the natural order, the more demonic it will be if it rebels" (96).

In Pam's case, her natural love for her son will be "buried" (killed) when she releases her claim on him and makes God her only desire. Apart from the grace of God, Pam's love for her son became fiercely possessive, even displacing God's claim on him. "He is mine, do you understand? Mine, mine, mine, for ever and ever." "How yours?" the Spirit asks, "You didn't make him" (GD 94).

Screwtape would see Pam as one of Hell's victories.

> The sense of ownership in general is always to be encouraged. The humans are always putting up claims to ownership which sound equally funny in Heaven and Hell, and we must keep them doing so... The word "mine" in its fully possessive sense cannot be uttered by a human being about anything. In the long run either Our Father or the Enemy will say "mine" of each thing that exists, and specially of each man. They will find out in the end, never fear, to whom their time, their souls, and their bodies really belong—certainly not to them, whatever happens (SL: 97-98)

By now, Lewis' head is swimming. How can he dare report that something as sacred and revered as the love of a mother can become demonic to the point of even finding fault with God? "They'd say I was inhuman: they'd say I believed in total depravity: they'd say I was attacking the best and the holiest things. They'd call me..." "It might do you no harm if they did," responds MacDonald, with a twinkle in his eye" (95).

MacDonald will not relent; Lewis must be courageous and stand for the truth even if his reputation suffers. And the truth is that no natural love can enter Heaven until it has been buried so that it may rise again. Can it be, asks Lewis, that Keats* was mistaken when he said that he was certain "of the holiness of the heart's affections?" "I doubt if he knew clearly what he meant," MacDonald replies, "but you and I must be clear. There is but one good; that is God. Everything else is good when it looks to Him and bad when it turns from Him. And the higher and mightier it is in the natural order, the more demonic it will be if it rebels" (96).

THE GHOST WITH THE RED LIZARD

MacDonald turns the attention of Lewis to a Ghost with dark, oily appearance. On the shoulder of the Ghost sits a small, red lizard, twitching its tail back and forth. For the first time, Lewis makes the sin (lust, in this case, according to MacDonald, p. 102) of a Ghost visible.

The lizard is whispering things into the ear of his host and doesn't stop even when the Ghost tells him to. The Ghost begins to smile under the onslaught, and turns to move away from the mountains. "Off so soon?" a voice asks, and Lewis finds himself in the presence of an angel so bright and hot that he seems to Lewis like the sun on a summer day (97). The Ghost explains to the Angel that he has brought the lizard on the condition that it remains silent, but since it won't stop talking, he has no choice but to leave.

The Angel offers to silence the lizard; an offer the Ghost gladly accepts, but then has second thoughts after learning the Angel plans to silence the lizard by killing it. He had something less drastic in mind; a gradual process should be enough to eventually control the lizard. No, the Angel insists, death is the only way. It must be now, and it will be painful, but it won't kill you. Finally, cursing and protesting, the Ghost gives his permission, realizing that even if the Angel does kill him, death would be better than living with the lizard on his shoulder.

The Angel seizes the lizard and ends its life, but to the amazement of Lewis, it begins to grow until a magnificent horse appears. Lewis is so transfixed by the sight that he misses out on another transformation: "I should have seen the actual completing of a man—an immense man, naked, not much smaller than the Angel" (100). Falling to the ground, the man embraces the feet of the "Burning One" and then rises, mounts the horse, and rides away toward the mountains with the speed of a shooting star.

At last—success. With only two more souls left (Sarah and Frank Smith), a passenger from the grey town finally chooses Heaven. The decision is agonizingly difficult, and the result painful but the transformation leaves no doubt that the resulting joy far outweighs any momentary suffering. Lewis celebrates Heaven's victory with a passage from the Psalms, and his conversation with MacDonald yields some important theology that needs a closer look.

UNDERSTANDING COMPLETE TRANSFORMATION

MacDonald asks Lewis if he has understood what he has seen, and emphasizes that when he reports the encounter, he must remember that the lizard became a horse only after it had been killed. But Lewis isn't sure he grasps the implications of the transformation. That something as base as lust could be changed would suggest that every part of a person can go to Heaven, even including the body and its appetites. Could that actually be true?

Yes, comes the answer, even the body will be changed. "It is sown a natural body, it is raised a spiritual body" (102, Lewis is quoting from 1 Cor 15:44). But, MacDonald cautions him, there is only one, unavoidable way: "flesh and blood cannot come to the Mountains." But God has not rejected the body: "Nothing, not even what is lowest and most bestial, will not be raised again if it submits to death. .... Lust (the lizard) is a poor, weak, whimpering thing compared with that richness and energy of desire which will arise when lust has been killed" (102).

"There was riding if you like!"

This is a significant change of focus. For the first time, the conversation between Lewis and MacDonald moves outside the context of the dream. Lewis has been concerned with the purification of the soul during the "time" between the death of the body and its resurrection. But now the conversation moves to "Flesh and blood," which is the Biblical way of referring to the physical body.

Lewis turns to the New Testament to emphasize to his readers that even the body must be transformed. Paul emphatically made this point when he wrote to the church at Corinth, where some did not believe that God would literally resurrect human bodies. He certainly will, Paul reminds them, but they will not be the same bodies as they were. Mortal bodies will be raised up and transformed into immortal bodies; bodies that were physical in nature will be given a spiritual nature (1 Cor 15:35-50). Then, these will be able to "come to the Mountains;" that is, into Heaven.

So, MacDonald in effect tells Lewis, there are two "problems" with humans. The first is sin, and the other is just being natural. What is natural is not sinful, but it belongs to this natural world, not Heaven. The natural can not bear the weight of glory that shall be revealed in Heaven. All that is natural must be transformed. "And where is your own body now? Didn't you know that Nature draws to an end?" Reginald asks his sister Pam (94).

HEAVEN'S CELEBRATION

Lewis then struggles with the fact that the man's lust was less an obstacle to divine grace than the excessive love of Pam for her son. But MacDonald corrects him, saying that she loved her son too little, not too much. Yes, he continues, mother-love is greater than lust, but that also means its corruption is greater than lust as well. And yet, if a weak thing like lust became such a glorious stallion, what would the risen form of maternal love have been?

As the transformed man rides away on his horse, instead of the lizard riding on him, the very landscape celebrates Heaven's success, the only victory Lewis sees in his dream. The song of the rejoicing elements proves to be Lewis's paraphrasing of the first four verses of Psalm 110. Jesus applied this Psalm to himself in debate with the Pharisees (Matt 22:41-46), but here Lewis uses it to describe Heaven's power to transform a sinful nature and the desire of the soul to be transformed. Lewis enjoyed using his poetic gifts to restate scriptures into modern language as the following comparison illustrates.

Psalm 110:1-4 *	Psalm 110:1-4 (Lewis)
The LORD says to my lord,	The Master says to our master,
"Sit at my right hand until I make your enemies your footstool."	Come up. Share my rest and splendour till all natures that were your enemies become slaves to dance before you and backs for you to ride, and firmness for your feet to rest on.
² The LORD sends out from Zion your mighty scepter. Rule in the midst of your foes.	From beyond all place and time, out of the very Place, authority will be given you: the strengths that once opposed your will shall be obedient fire in your blood and Heavenly thunder in your voice.
³ Your people will offer themselves willingly on the day you lead your forces on the holy mountains. From the womb of the morning, like dew, your youth will come to you.	Overcome us that, so overcome, we may be ourselves: we desire the beginning of your reign as we desire dawn and dew, wetness at the birth of light.
⁴ The LORD has sworn and will not change his mind, "You are a priest forever according to the order of Melchizedek."	Master, your Master has appointed you for ever: to be our King of Justice and our high priest.

*NRSV

CHAPTER 12

Sarah Smith and Frank

The discussion of lust and maternal love comes to an end when Lewis is distracted by light dancing everywhere in the forest. Soon a wondrous sight indeed comes into view. This elaborate introduction of the final fictitious person (and her husband) after the powerful account of the first and only Ghost to accept the pain of sanctification in order to enter Heaven is Lewis's way of signaling the climax of the journey. Something, and someone, wonderful is approaching, and the descriptive powers of Lewis reach new heights.

Wondering if he is seeing the reflection of water in another river, Lewis soon realizes a procession is approaching: a pageant in honor of a woman of inexpressible beauty. She may be clothed or naked; Lewis isn't sure since both seem true, and he finds himself unable to recall her beauty, which is his way of saying any description he could provide would fall short. Dancing Spirits come first, then boys and girls, musicians, and the lady herself. After her is a procession of men and women, followed by more animals than Lewis can count.

Lewis is "pulling out all the stops" here, as he struggles (eloquently) to describe her glory and beauty. Everything about the lady and her train is permeated with divine life: "If I could remember their singing and write down the notes, no man who read that score would ever grow sick or old" (104-105). And to the astonishment of Lewis, MacDonald informs him that "Already there is joy enough in the little finger of a great saint such as yonder lady to waken all the dead things of the universe into life" (106-107).

In this longest of all encounters, so important that Lewis divided it into two chapters, the focus is equally divided between a Ghost (Frank) and his wife, the glorified Sarah Smith from Golders Green*, who was a nobody on earth, but one of the greatest in Heaven. Frank is also a sight to behold, though for a very different reason. Who can not be appalled at the pride which can look full in the face of Heaven's beauty embodied in a loved one, and still turn away? As Lewis watches them interact, he realizes that the real Frank is a dwarf who is leading on a chain a tall Ghost with a black hat. Searching his memory, Lewis finally places him: "He was like a seedy actor of the old school" (107).

Sarah ignores the Tragedian, Frank's façade that represents his self-pity, and speaks only to the Dwarf, who is having a very difficult time coming to grips with Sarah's condition. Sarah isn't unhappy, as he would prefer, hasn't missed him, as he had hoped, and he takes that to mean she doesn't care. She asks his forgiveness for all she ever did wrong, and invites him into eternal joy, but he instead recalls the time she took the last stamp to write to her mother. If only she had noticed his unselfishness.

The final blow to his ego comes when she tells him he is not needed. "What needs could I have," she said, "now that I have all? I am full now, not empty. I am in Love Himself, not lonely.... You shall be the same. Come and see. We shall have no *need* for one another now: we can begin to love truly" (111).

I DO NOT KNOW THAT I EVER SAW ANYTHING MORE TERRIBLE THAN
THE STRUGGLE OF THAT DWARF GHOST AGAINST JOY.

CHAPTER 13

The Struggle for Frank's Soul

As the Psalmist used the word "selah" to invite his readers to stop and reflect, so Lewis takes the unusual step of abruptly interrupting the dialogue between Frank and Sarah by ending one chapter and beginning another. The device works; Lewis seems to be holding his breath with his readers as Frank struggles against joy and is nearly overcome. "Somewhere, incalculable ages ago, there must have been gleams of humour and reason in him" (113).

Sarah's joy and love storm the fortress of Frank's hardened heart. How can he possibly resist? "For one moment... he saw the absurdity of the Tragedian... But the light that reached him, reached him against his will" (113). He will not stop trying to make others miserable by having them pity him. But in Heaven, Sarah is beyond his reach. "Everything becomes more and more itself. Here is joy that cannot be shaken. Our light can swallow up your darkness: but your darkness cannot now infect our light" (116).

As she pleads with Frank to stop using pity to blackmail others, he shrinks until he is too small to be seen. Lewis isn't sure, but he thinks the actor swallowed up Frank, chain and all. Previously he saw a grumbling woman who was in danger of becoming nothing more than an unending grumble; now that terrible possibility becomes true even while he watches. Frank refuses to let go of his façade, and so Frank disappears, leaving only the facade.

Since only the Tragedian remains, for the first time Sarah addresses him. "I never knew you. Perhaps you had better leave me" (116). The Tragedian vanishes, and Sarah returns to her company of Bright Spirits who welcome her back with Lewis's version of Psalm 91.

Psalm 91 *	Psalm 91 (Lewis)
You who live in the shelter of the Most High, who abide in the shadow of the Almighty, 2 will say to the LORD, "My refuge and my fortress; my God, in whom I trust."	The Happy Trinity is her home: nothing can trouble her joy.
3 For he will deliver you from the snare of the fowler and from the deadly pestilence;	She is the bird that evades every net: the wild deer that leaps every pitfall.
4 he will cover you with his pinions, and under his wings you will find refuge; his faithfulness is a shield and buckler.	Like the mother bird to its chickens or a shield to the arm'd knight: so is the Lord to her mind, in His unchanging lucidity.
5 You will not fear the terror of the night, or the arrow that flies by day,	Bogies will not scare her in the dark: bullets will not frighten her in the day. Falsehoods tricked out as truths assail her in vain: she sees through the lie as if it were glass.
6 or the pestilence that stalks in darkness, or the destruction that wastes at noonday.	The invisible germ will not harm her: nor yet the glittering sunstroke.
7 A thousand may fall at your side, ten thousand at your right hand, but it will not come near you. 8 You will only look with your eyes and see the punishment of the wicked. 9 Because you have made the LORD your refuge, the Most High your dwelling place, 10 no evil shall befall you, no scourge come near your tent.	A thousand fail to solve the problem, ten thousand choose the wrong turning: but she passes safely through.

11 For he will command his angels concerning you to guard you in all your ways.	He details immortal gods to attend her: upon every road where she must travel.
12 On their hands they will bear you up, so that you will not dash your foot against a stone.	They take her hand at hard places: she will not stub her toes in the dark.
13 You will tread on the lion and the adder, the young lion and the serpent you will trample under foot.	She may walk among Lions and rattlesnakes: among dinosaurs and nurseries of lionets.
14 Those who love me, I will deliver; I will protect those who know my name. 15 When they call to me, I will answer them; I will be with them in trouble, I will rescue them and honor them. 16 With long life I will satisfy them, and show them my salvation.	He fills her brim full with immensity of life: he leads her to see the world's desire.

* NRSV

CHAPTER 14

The Chessboard Vision

Now the dream is nearly over and Lewis is left alone with his tour guide once again. The final dialogue (which includes a vision) between Lewis and his tour guide brings the discussion of human choice to a close just as the appearance of Sarah Smith was the final and most moving scene of the book. Drama and discussion, intertwined throughout, now reach a climax together.

As the music fades away, Lewis finds that he is troubled by what he has seen. The plight of Frank has not affected Sarah in the least. And so he asks, "Is it really tolerable that she should be untouched by his misery, even his self-made misery" (117)? Lewis knows that he represents many, perhaps millions, who have been troubled by the thought of tormented souls in Hell. "What some people say on earth is that the final loss of one soul gives the lie to all the joy of those who are saved" (118). MacDonald reminds him that what he has just seen shows that this is not the case, and explains why Frank cannot change her:

> Son, son, it must be one way or the other. Either the day must come when joy prevails and all the makers of misery are no longer able to infect it: or else for ever and ever the makers of misery can destroy in others the happiness they reject for themselves. I know it has a grand sound to say ye'll accept no salvation which leaves even one creature in the dark outside. But watch that sophistry or ye'll make a Dog* in the Manger the tyrant of the universe (118).

What Lewis is saying through MacDonald has been portrayed in every dialogue. Heaven was ready to redeem even the worst passengers from the bus, showing that the "action of pity" lives on into eternity. But not the "passion of pity;" that compassion good people instinctively feel for the suffering of others. When people choose that suffering, resisting the offer of goodness, compassion or pity is no longer in order. Stated bluntly, the only people in Hell are those who choose to be there. Since the presence of God would be unbearable to them, God allows them to have what they choose, rather than force Himself upon anyone. So God is just. And to be just to everyone, He does not allow those who reject Him to affect the joy of the rest. There is still, however, the larger problem of those who have never heard the good news of the Gospel; what of their choices? What chance do they have? Will the justice of God extend even to them? The answers Lewis gives are the subject of Part III.

Meanwhile, as Lewis reaches the end of his dream, he also comes to the limits of his theology. MacDonald earlier explained that Lewis was given this dream so that he could observe people choosing their eternal destiny. But now, Lewis finds that freedom of choice leads to a curious result. If humans really do have that freedom, and Lewis believes they do, he will not be able to find the answer to the ultimate question: who will be saved? Some theologians already have decided that in the end, everyone will be saved, but MacDonald refuses to confirm this position, even though he himself had the reputation of being a Universalist (121). Why? Because if we now know that all will be saved, the freedom to refuse Heaven is gone.

In the same way, MacDonald explains, if predestination is true and only some will be saved at the end of time, then the freedom to choose Heaven is denied to some. "For every attempt to see the shape of eternity except through the lens of Time destroys your knowledge of Freedom... Ye *cannot* know eternal reality by a definition. Time itself, and all acts and events that fill Time, are the definition, and it must be lived" (122).

Lewis feels so strongly about this supreme human prerogative that he reinforces the explanation of MacDonald in words by means of a vision so that he can visually portray his theology of choice.

> ...Suddenly all was changed. I saw a great assembly of gigantic forms all motionless, all in deepest silence, standing forever about a little silver table and looking upon it. And on the table there were little figures like chessmen who went to and fro doing this and that... And these chessmen are men and women as they appear to themselves and to one another in this world. And the silver table is Time. And those who stand and watch are the immortal souls of those same men and women (123).

In the vision, the little chess pieces represented people in mortal bodies living out their earthly existence ("doing this and that") while their immortal souls watch. Lewis (and many others) conveyed the same idea using the metaphor of actors acting out their roles on stage while the real world lies concealed behind the curtains. No matter which metaphor is used, the point is the same. The "real world" (the real Narnia) is not this physical world but the spirit world where immortal souls will someday go for good or ill; praise or judgment. One of the benefits of prayer, Lewis says, is that it reminds me "that this 'real world' and 'real self' are very far from being rock-bottom realities" (LTM: 81).

Chapter 15

Summary of Part I
The "Sociology" of *The Great Divorce*

THE CHOICE OF EVERY SOUL

Lewis encountered quite a variety of people; male and female, average and gifted. Some were completely centered upon themselves while others, in the spirit of service, were dedicated to the reform of the grey town. Yet all twenty of them had in common a two-part challenge; they must own up to their sins, and then allow God to remove them. Heaven stands ready to help, but most of them returned to the bus. In the words of MacDonald: "There is always something they insist on keeping, even at the price of misery" (69). And, I would add, even at the cost of joy.

Every conversation between the Ghosts and those who met them sustains Lewis' contention that there is no marriage between Heaven and Hell; in fact, not even the smallest compromise is possible. Lewis knew many have been moved by a sense of pity for the lost, and he included several well-intentioned Ghosts in the dialogues who were prepared to bring Heaven down into Hell. The Poet believed Hell would benefit from more intellectual life. Ikey was prepared to reform the place by economic benefits. And the Episcopal Ghost rejected Ikey's approach (too materialistic) in favor of theological reform. All these are destined to failure, as human history as shown. "Crude salvationism" is the world's only hope.

Nor can the "marriage" be accomplished by bringing Hell up into Heaven. The solid Spirits are not affected by the Ghosts who arrive filled with filth, vituperation, hatred, spite and (ridiculous) suggestions to kill the animals, pave over the sharp grass, and dam up the river. The Ghosts stand ready to help with Heaven's reform, but they are the ones who need the change. And, oddly enough, even some of these, MacDonald reports, do accept that help. But help comes only on Heaven's terms; Heaven will not change to suit them.

UNDERSTANDING SANCTIFICATION

There are two common errors people make about sanctification that Lewis was careful to guard against. The first misconception is that when God puts to death the sinful aspects of the soul, those aspects disappear. But soul "surgery" is more complicated than the physical surgery that simply removes diseased tissues. Every evil is a distorted form of what was originally created good, and once a distortion has been cured, the goodness can be restored. When the Lustful Ghost allowed the angel to kill the lizard on his shoulder, the lizard became a magnificent stallion, symbolizing genuine love no longer stunted by lust. In the words of Lewis: "Every natural love will rise again and live forever in this country: but none will rise again until it has been buried" (96).

The second error is to assume that when believers are finally conformed to the image of Christ, they become clones. Since sanctification restores the full person, the opposite is true. In fact, Lewis asserts, those who have chosen to worship self rather than God are the ones who become more and more alike. Unlike evil, which eventually fashions souls into self-centered beings, goodness branches out until every redeemed soul reaches its unique, God-given potential.

Lewis compared the divine life in a person to salt, which brings out the flavor in foods. "It is something like that with Christ and us. The more we get what we now call 'ourselves' out of the way and let Him take us over, the more truly ourselves we become" (MC 174). This is why the Spirit promised the artist "When you've grown into a Person... there'll be some things which you'll see better than anyone else. One of the things you'll want to do will be to tell us about them. But not yet" (79). Or in the words of Sarah Smith, "Everything becomes more and more itself" (116).

So then, Heaven ultimately exalts the uniqueness of each individual, but only after each individual has fully surrendered the self to its Creator. Then, once purified, God gives back what he originally placed within each human so that it can truly and selflessly fulfill its original purpose. "If grace perfects nature it must expand all our natures into the full richness of the diversity which God intended when He made them, and Heaven will display far more variety than Hell" (LTM: 10). Lewis observed the same variety in living things here on earth. "Even on the biological level life is not like a pool but like a tree. It does not move towards unity but away from it and the creatures grow further apart as they increase in perfection. Good, as it ripens, becomes continually more different not only from evil but from other good" (10).

In the case of the artist, his ability to depict how nature reflected the Creator was degraded over time until it became simply the means of establishing his reputation. Bringing glory to God and helping others do so through his painting ceased to be his goal. But, the Spirit promised, when his pride has been removed, that God-given talent will once again allow him to see "better than anyone else." So, Lewis concludes, the removal of sins allows the real person to appear, and since each person is unique, God is glorified by all the diversity that reflects him in so many different ways. "From the highest to the lowest, self exists to be abdicated, and, by that abdication, becomes the more truly self…" (PP: 152).

> Heaven is a city, and a Body, because the blessed remain eternally different: a society, because each has something to tell all the others—fresh and ever fresh news of the "My God" who each finds in Him whom all praise as "Our God." For doubtless the continually successful, yet never completed, attempt by each soul to communicate its unique vision to all others (and that by means whereof earthly art and philosophy are but clumsy imitations) is also among the ends for which the individual was created (PP: 150).

KEEPING THINGS SIMPLE

Paul wrote "we see in a mirror dimly" (1 Cor 13:12) and this is certainly true regarding sanctification. How does God know what each soul needs? And how does he cleanse and perfect a soul? Does he do the work himself, or, as Lewis depicted, does he work through angels and even human spirits people once knew on earth? If there is more than one sin in a human soul, does God remove them one at a time, is permission required each time, or is one "general" permission enough? And do souls actively participate in postmortem sanctification, as on earth, or is a passive "go ahead" enough?

Lewis knows better than to get into such questions which the Scriptures do not answer, and he would be upset if his vivid, imaginative descriptions were taken as the literal truth. What Lewis does know is that the all-knowing God surely understands what must die in order to be reborn, the all-powerful God is able to accomplish that, and the most holy God will not be satisfied until the work is complete. But each person must yield; Heaven must be chosen, desired and achieved only by God's grace.

Will he use others? The Bible doesn't say. There is one enigmatic passage that might hint at this: Jesus advised his listeners to imitate the unscrupulous steward who put others in his debt when he knew his master was about to fire him. He prepared for his future, and it would be wise to use "mammon" (money or resources) to prepare for the inevitability of death. "And I say to you, make friends for yourselves by means of the mammon of unrighteousness; that when it fails, they may receive you into the eternal dwellings" (Luke 16:9). But the text does not reveal whether such friends will be instruments of divine grace.

In a way, Lewis had no choice but to depict God using others, given his emphasis upon the infinite distance between Heaven and Hell. The glory of God is so great, and the souls of those in the grey town are so nearly nothing, direct contact is impossible. Only the faintest, most indirect expressions of the divine presence can be tolerated, and sometimes not even those. Even before the Spirits arrive from the heights of Heaven, every blade of grass, every golden apple and drop of water confronts the Ghosts with solid reality in all of its beauty and terror. To that landscape I now turn.

Part II

The "Geography" of The Great Divorce

CHAPTER ONE

The Grey Town

We've reached the place I told thee to expect,
Where thou shouldst see the miserable race,
Those who have lost the good of intellect.
(*Hell*, Canto iii. 16-18: 85)

BOTLEY

Late in the winter term of 1916, Lewis made his first trip to the town of Oxford to sit for his scholarship examination. His first impression upon leaving the train was disappointing, but he took it in stride since "Towns always show their worst face to the railway" (SBJ: 184). Setting off in anticipation of the "dreaming spires" of the university, his disappointment grew. The city of Oxford was much larger than he expected, and he began to ask himself "Could this dreary succession of mean shops really be Oxford?" Not until he began to reach open country did he turn around to see, far away, the spires and towers of Oxford University. "I had come out of the station on the wrong side and been all this time walking into what was even then the mean and sprawling suburb of Botley" (SBJ: 184).

Lewis took this "adventure" of heading off in the wrong direction to be an allegory of his whole life, and his experience of anxiety and then relief on that cold winter day left a permanent mark on his memory. Botley now has the dubious honor of being the model for the grey town, or Hell, in *The Great Divorce*. Once again, but fortunately now only in a dream, Lewis finds himself wandering in "mean streets," seeing no one, and never coming to a better part of town. Instead, there was an endless succession of dingy lodging houses, tobacco stores, and "bookshops of the sort that sell *The Works of Aristotle*" (13). Time seems frozen in "that dismal moment when only a few shops have lit up and it is not yet dark enough for their windows to look cheering" (13). And a misty, unceasing drizzle completes the gloomy picture.

What a place! But is it really Hell? For millennia, fire, brimstone and the suffering of the wicked have been the stock depictions of the place, and many Scriptures agree. And yet, there are many similar (and even worse) places on earth like Botley where people live and call home. The Hard-Bitten Ghost was disappointed that he had not encountered "red fire and devils and all sorts of interesting people sizzling on grids" but Lewis constructed this landscape, both time and place, to convey his belief that the souls here are in an intermediate state of being; between Heaven and Hell, and between the death of the body and its resurrection. Even the color of the town is somewhere between white and black. And so he breaks with long-standing tradition by designing a setting that would reflect his personal view of Hell that is not quite Hell, but eventually will be.

Lewis also intended the description of the grey town/Botley to express his conviction that life on earth *before* death is also, in a sense, an intermediate state of being, since it's not too late to make the choices that will eventually lead to Hell or Heaven. "Earth, I think, will not be found by anyone to be in the end a very distinct place. I think earth, if chosen instead of Heaven, will turn out to have been, all along, only a region in Hell: and earth, if put second to Heaven, to have been from the beginning a part of Heaven itself" (11).

LIFE IN THE GREY TOWN

One of the first impressions of the grey town is that it is a place of deadness; dead or dying minds, dead or dying souls. It is a place where curiosity has been forever squelched and self-satisfaction has closed the door to any desire for the development that reflection and education can bring. The shops and cinemas are all the citizens care about, complains the Poet Ghost. "The appalling lack of any intellectual life doesn't worry *them*" (16). The Episcopal Ghost hopes his Theological Society will bring some mental stimulation, but even this optimistic soul must admit to "a certain lack of grip—a certain confusion of mind" (46).

Later in the dream, Lewis himself perceives that the crowds of souls who came up on the bus to give Heaven a piece of their mind were "all equally incurious about the country in which they had arrived. They repelled every attempt to teach them, and when they found that nobody listened to them they went back, one by one, to the bus" (76). Earthly slums like Botley leave their mark on those who live in them, but Lewis is suggesting the opposite is also true. The grey town is what it is because it reflects the spiritual condition of those who have chosen to stay there.

THE SIZE OF THE GREY TOWN

Lewis also takes pains to impress the reader with the vastness and emptiness of the grey town. In his dream he wanders for hours without meeting anyone, and the dreary shops and lodging houses stretch on endlessly. Even when the bus begins to rise above the ground no end to the town appears, and he learns from the Intelligent Man that some residents are millions of miles or even light years away from the bus stop. Some of the older souls are "so far off by now that they could never think of coming to the bus stop at all. Astronomical distances" (21).

After the quarrel on the bus, Lewis learns more about the grey town from the new person in the seat next to him. The reason the place seems so empty, Ikey explains, is that people constantly quarrel with one another and when they do, they move somewhere else. Not only that, they only need to think of a house and it appears. And so the town is constantly expanding, since people can't get along. Not only do those moving toward Hell refuse personal growth, they also have abandoned social skills. The two are related; one says "I'm satisfied with what I know" and the other "I'm satisfied with what I am; it's *your* fault we can't get along."

Quarrels! Everyone has them, but quarrels are not just a minor problem for Lewis. In fact, when he began the logical progression of thought that would demonstrate all mankind's need of salvation, he started *Mere Christianity* with this very topic. Quarrels arise when someone feels wronged by someone else, and Lewis took them as evidence that people everywhere have an inner standard of right and wrong. But in the grey town, the other person is always at fault and moving away is better than forgiving or asking forgiveness in hopes of reconciliation.

Lewis portrays Heaven's perspective when the Big Ghost meets Len, his employee back on earth, who murdered Jack, a mutual acquaintance. But that wasn't the worst, Len confesses. "I murdered you in my heart, deliberately, for years" (35). The act was never carried out, but the desire to murder was there, and so Len was sent to ask his forgiveness and to serve him. Heaven demands reconciliation between quarreling humans as well as between God and man. "So if you are offering your gift at the altar, and there remember that your brother has something against you, leave your gift there before the altar and go; first be reconciled to your brother, and then come and offer your gift" (Matt 5:23-24).

Ultimately, the person who won't forgive others will even hold a grudge against God Himself. After all, isn't He running the show? When things go wrong, shouldn't He fix them, or, better yet, shouldn't He have prevented them if He loves the humans he created so much? God took Michael from Pam, his mother, to deliver him from her overbearing control. God allows, Lewis implies, tragic events on earth to achieve through them his higher purposes. But Pam chooses Hell rather than accept God's will, since that would mean acknowledging she was wrong to try to possess someone else. "No one has a right to come between me and my son. Not even God" (93). If she refuses to end her quarrel with God she will have sealed her own fate.

Lewis is using the concept of physical space, or places, of this world, to describe conditions in the spirit world, just as Jesus depicted the spiritual conditions of the rich man and Lazarus not by telling us how moral or immoral they were but by placing them in very different environments; one with fire and torment, and the other with physical comforts and companionship. When Lewis described the bus stop as being a great distance from the Civic Center, he was implying that people who let daily life crowd out spiritual priorities will find it increasingly difficult to reverse that trend and move toward God. At first a soul may resist change, but in the end change becomes impossible; the bus stop of God's grace will be clean out of sight.

BUILDING HOUSES IN THE GREY TOWN

The souls in the grey town are preoccupied with self above all else. No longer interested in learning about themselves or getting along with others, they project all blame upon others and even God. Only the self, now isolated, remains. Lewis chooses a very interesting way to portray this personality sickness: people live in houses they construct simply by thinking of them. In the case of Napoleon, who ignored the authority of the Church and crowned himself Emperor of France, he has constructed for himself a huge house (to match his huge ego) built in the Empire style.

When the Intelligent Man tells Lewis that the houses don't keep out the rain, he asks (in a wonderful double entendre) "What the devil is the use of building them, then" (24)? For "safety," the Ghost replies. This is wishful thinking, of course; a house that can't keep out the rain won't offer protection from anything else. But the illogic captures the essence of Hell, where houses are a façade or a projection of what the souls would like themselves and reality to be.

WEATHER IN THE GREY TOWN

Is there no hope in the grey town? Some souls did get on the bus and at least one did not return. Change is still possible, at least for some. And there may be one aspect of life in the grey town that (in my opinion, at least) represents the grace of God, even "down there." The rain never stops, and the houses that souls build just by thinking of them are not able, Lewis learns from Ikey, to keep the water out. In this way, God provides a constant reminder; a warning, in fact, that their facades are only illusions. Those who have a desire for reality, however weak, will find their way to the bus stop; those who do not will eventually cease to mind the rain.

Time in the Grey Town

Mulling over the Intelligent Man's explanation that people built houses for their safety (24), Lewis wonders why safety is a concern in the grey town. Ikey reluctantly, in a whisper, explains that time will not always stand still there; night is coming. Lewis doesn't see the connection between nightfall and safety. "Well," says Ikey, "No one wants to be out of doors when it becomes dark." "Why not?" Lewis wants to know. Ikey's whispers his response to Lewis to avoid upsetting the other passengers. But Lewis persists, angering the others: "Who are 'They'"? I asked. "And what are you afraid they'll do to you? And why should they come out when it's dark? And what protection could an imaginary house give if there was any danger" (24)?

The sudden reluctance on the part of Lewis to say what he's thinking (only here) and the capitalized "They" suggest something significant is afoot. Since the book ends with morning coming "up there," dusk must have turned to night "down there." And since by morning Lewis means (as we shall see) the resurrection, he has in mind what follows the resurrection: humanity standing before Christ at the Last Judgment. That judgment is not restricted to humanity but angels as well. In the Parable of the Sheep and the Goats (a parable that Lewis referred to many times): "Then he will say to those at his left hand, 'You that are accursed, depart from me into the eternal fire prepared for the devil and his angels'" (Matt 25:41 NRSV; Rev 20:10 describes the actual casting of Satan into the lake of fire.). Given who "They" are, and since Lewis has described their agenda so well in *The Screwtape Letters* ("To us a human is primarily food; our aim is the absorption of its will into ours... Our war aim is a world in which Our Father Below has drawn all other beings into himself" SL: 37-38.), the reluctance of Lewis to get into the unpleasant details of what will happen when the devil and his angels are cast into Hell is quite understandable. And if the houses can't even keep out the rain...

Time therefore is of the essence; dawn (the light of the Second Coming) will break and bring with it night "below," with all of its terrors and the message of "too late". Dusk and dawn will vanish; only Heaven and Hell will remain. Before then, souls must yield to Heaven so the process of purification can begin. "Natural loves can hope for eternity only in so far as they have allowed themselves to be taken into the eternity of Charity; have at least allowed the process to begin here on earth, *before the night comes when no man can work*" (FL: 136-137; emphasis mine).

CHAPTER TWO

Between Hell and Heaven

THE ABYSS

Hours after they leave the ground, light begins to filter into the bus until the gray skies become gloriously blue. "We seemed to be floating in a pure vacancy. There were no lands, so sun, no stars in sight: only the radiant Abyss" (26). Now that the grey town is no longer visible, Lewis opens a window and begins to breathe the wonderful fresh air. But the passengers shout at him as if he were letting in the plague, and the Intelligent Man reaches across him and pulls the window back up.

In the new, stronger light, Lewis looks around at the passengers. "They were all fixed faces, full not of possibilities but of impossibilities, some gaunt, some bloated, some glaring with idiotic ferocity; some drowned beyond recovery in dreams; but all, in one way or another, distorted and faded. One had a feeling that they might fall to pieces at any moment if the light grew much stronger" (26). Even in the subdued light of the Abyss, the spiritual condition of the passengers—their faces reveal their souls—becomes obvious... and yet, they did get on the bus... perhaps for some there still is hope.

But what is the significance of this strange place in Lewis' dream; the "radiant Abyss" that separates the grey town from the outskirts of Heaven? The idea comes from the scriptures; specifically The Parable of the Rich Man and Lazarus, found only in the Gospel of Luke. Since this parable is one of the very few glimpses Jesus gives into the afterlife, here is the full text:

> [19] "There was a rich man who was dressed in purple and fine linen and who feasted sumptuously every day. [20] And at his gate lay a poor man named Lazarus, covered with sores, [21] who longed to satisfy his hunger with what fell from the rich man's table; even the dogs would come and lick his sores. [22] The poor man died and was carried away by the angels to be with Abraham. The rich man also died and was buried. [23] In Hades, where he was being tormented, he looked up and saw Abraham

far away with Lazarus by his side. [24] He called out, 'Father Abraham, have mercy on me, and send Lazarus to dip the tip of his finger in water and cool my tongue; for I am in agony in these flames.' [25] But Abraham said, 'Child, remember that during your lifetime you received your good things, and Lazarus in like manner evil things; but now he is comforted here, and you are in agony.

[26] Besides all this, *between you and us a great chasm has been fixed*, so that those who might want to pass from here to you cannot do so, and no one can cross from there to us.'

[27] He said, 'Then, father, I beg you to send him to my father's house—[28] for I have five brothers—that he may warn them, so that they will not also come into this place of torment.' [29] Abraham replied, 'They have Moses and the prophets; they should listen to them.' [30] He said, 'No, father Abraham; but if someone goes to them from the dead, they will repent.' [31] He said to him, 'If they do not listen to Moses and the prophets, neither will they be convinced even if someone rises from the dead.'" (Luke 16:19-31 NRSV)

Lewis took more from this passage than just the idea of an Abyss or chasm. Note that Jesus depicted conditions in the spirit world in earthly terms; the rich man wants water for his tongue, even though he is deceased and no longer in a body. From the way spiritual places are depicted in Biblical passages, Lewis concluded that "Heaven is, by definition, outside our experience, but all intelligible descriptions must be of things within our experience" ("Weight of Glory" in WG: 33). And so Lewis depicts both Hell and Heaven in earthly terms to communicate his theology, not the actual "landscapes."

Abraham refused the Rich Man's request for water because the "great chasm" prevented souls from leaving their "compartment" (which reflects their spiritual condition) and visiting another. "Then no one can ever reach them?" asks Lewis, concerned about this seemingly insurmountable barrier. MacDonald replies (giving Lewis's position): "Only the Greatest of all can make Himself small enough to enter Hell. For the higher a thing is, the lower it can descend–a man can sympathise with a horse but a horse cannot sympathise with a rat. Only One has descended into Hell" (121). Thanks to Christ, souls are longer confined to a compartment in Hades.

Nevertheless, it is an Abyss, and described as "great" in the parable. Lewis never reveals how rapidly the bus is moving, but the chasm takes "hours" to cross and no bottom or top can be seen (25). Again, Lewis uses a vast distance in the literal sense to represent the spiritual distance between souls in Hell and souls in Heaven. People who have fled from reality for all or most of their lives must travel a great distance, spiritually speaking, to reach even the outskirts of Heaven. And they do so only by getting on the bus, which raises an interesting question. Just who is the bus driver, and what does the bus represent?

THE BUS DRIVER* AND THE BUS

The bus and its driver as Lewis describes them are certainly out of place in the drab grey town. "It was a wonderful vehicle, blazing with golden light, heraldically coloured. The Driver himself seemed full of light and he only used one hand to steer with. The other he waved before his face as if to fan away the greasy steam of the rain" (15). The reaction of the passengers, at least those who haven't already quarreled and left the line, is predictably negative. "Looks as if *he* had a good time of it, eh?" "My dear, why can't he behave *naturally*?" "All that gilding and purple, I call it a wicked waste." Lewis himself can't see what the fuss is all about: "I could see nothing in the countenance of the Driver to justify all this, unless it were that he had a look of authority and seemed intent on carrying out his job" (15).

Just who is this bus driver? One might expect from the scriptures and from MacDonald's words to Lewis, "Only One has descended into Hell," (121) that Christ Himself is at the wheel, but this is not so. Lewis follows the example of Dante, who made it clear that his journey into Hell, Purgatory and Heaven was possible only because Christ had already come and gone. Christ never makes an appearance in Lewis's dream. So then who is the driver?

Let's look for clues in Dante's *Comedy*. In Canto VIII of the *Inferno* (Hell), Phlegyas* ferries Dante and Virgil over the river Styx* so they can reach the city of Dis*. When they arrive there, Virgil speaks to the two fallen angels who stand guard at the gates, and they offer him entrance but coldly leave Dante to find his way back alone. Dante is crushed, knowing he will never succeed.

> Reader, do but conceive of my dismay,
> Hearing these dreadful words! It seemed quite plain
> I nevermore should see the light of day.
> (*Hell*, Canto VIII; 94-96, 118.)

Virgil refuses to enter Dis without Dante, and so the arrogant angels shut him out as well. But he encourages Dante, confident that help is coming. Sure enough, a mighty angel comes with a noise like thunder, opens the gate with a touch of his wand and rebukes the fallen angels for resisting God's will. Note how the approach of this angel is described as Virgil points Dante toward their approaching rescuer:

> He loosed my eyes: "Now look," said he, "see there,
> Yonder, beyond the foam of the ancient lake,
> Where the harsh marsh mist hangs thickest upon the air."

And as the frogs, spying the foeman snake,
>Go squattering over the pond, and dive, and sit
>Huddled in the mud, even so I saw them break

Apart, whole shoals of ruined spirits, and flit
>Scudding from the path of one who came to us,
>Walking the water of Styx with unwet feet.

His left hand, moving, fanned away the gross
>Air from his face, nor elsewise did he seem
>At all to find the way laborious.
And when I saw him, right well did I deem
>Him sent from Heaven, and turned me to my guide,
>Who signed me to be still and bow to him.

What scorn was in his look! He stood beside
>The gate, and touched it with a wand; it flew
>Open; there was no resistance; all stood wide.
>(*Hell*, Canto IX; 73-90, p. 125.)

The description by both Dante and Lewis of the figure waving one hand before his face to fan away the bad air seems specific enough to conclude that Lewis, like Dante, brought an unnamed angel to the rescue of those souls who would leave the grey town. But Lewis gives other angels, and perfected human Spirits, greater roles to play than did Dante (except for Beatrice). Now that Christ has opened the way, the angels and Spirits who serve Him continue the work of sanctification as they come to meet the passengers on the bus.

This leaves the bus itself, blazing with golden light and brightly colored. Since it is the means by which souls can leave the grey town, it represents the "vehicle" of divine grace as its description implies. The bus, its driver, the Spirits who come to meet the Ghosts, and the Burning Angel who helped the Ghost with a lizard on his shoulder are all ways Lewis chose to express how Heaven uses its citizens to partner with Christ for the sanctification of human souls.

CHAPTER THREE

Heaven

Those happy men of yore who sang the golden time
And all its happy state—maybe indeed
They on Parnassus dreamed of this fair clime.

Here was the innocent root of all man's seed;
Here spring is endless, here all fruits are, here
The nectar is, which runs in all their rede.

(*Purgatory*, Canto xxviii. 139-144: 293)

CONDITION OR PLACE?

The Bible speaks of several different places in the spirit world: Tartarus, Hades, Paradise, the Third Heaven, and so on. Theologians do not agree on whether these are symbols or literal "places" in the spirit world; but most do agree that the descriptions of these places are not to be taken literally. Rather, such features as fire, suffering, pearly gates and streets of gold, a feast, a temple indicate the spirituality, or lack of it, of those who dwell there. Let's remain open to the possibility that there are many places or "environments" within the spirit world, just as there are in the physical world. In fact, I wouldn't be surprised if there are many more places in the spirit world than in ours. But let's go to the authoritative source; what did Jesus say?

We've already considered the parable of The Rich Man and Lazarus (with Abraham) who were in different compartments because they were in different spiritual conditions. Jesus also told his disciples that there were many "rooms" in "my Father's house" and that he was leaving them so he could prepare a place for them where they could be with him—perhaps the place he would prepare was one of those rooms or dwelling places in his Father's house (John 14:2-3). See also "Paradise" in Appendix III for the evidence that this place Jesus prepared was the Paradise promised to the thief on the cross, and the place which Paul was privileged to visit.

And a "paradise" of natural beauty is precisely how Lewis chose to depict the outskirts of Heaven. Whereas the grey town was urban slums, Heaven is green, pastoral countryside. No mean streets, petty shops, or quarreling neighbors. The landscape here reflects the cleansed souls of the Spirits who belong here. What a contrast the unchanged passengers make as they curse and strike each other in their attempt to get out of the bus first. Finally Lewis is left alone on the bus. Through the door comes fresh air and the singing of a lark. He steps out into the coolness of a summer day just before dawn... a Paradise indeed. And yet...

DESCRIBING HEAVEN

The bus ride is really more like a trip in an airplane; the first indication that the trip has begun is when they leave the ground. Hours pass until the grey town is no longer visible, and the vehicle is floating in the radiant Abyss. Finally, a cliff can be seen, so high that Lewis is not able to see the bottom. "We were mounting all the time" (27). The bus finally stops in level, grassy country with a wide river running through it.

Christ may have prepared a Paradise for us, but the Scriptures give no description of the place. So where did Lewis get his ideas? Actually, for millennia people in many cultures have imagined a beautiful, pastoral setting to be enjoyed by souls that have lived good lives. The Elysian fields of Greek mythology is one example. (See "Golden Apples" in Appendix E). Perhaps we need look no farther than Dante, who envisioned Purgatory as a mountain with seven levels, corresponding to the Seven Deadly Sins. Just above the highest level of Purgatory (lust) is the earthly Paradise from which Adam and Eve were expelled. From there, cleansed souls journey into the higher levels of Heaven.

The differences between the grey town and the outskirts of Heaven are obvious. But less obvious is the paradox arising from the way Lewis described them. Paradise is painfully sharp and dangerously solid, while the dreary streets below are relatively comfortable to those who dwell there. In this way, Lewis again emphasizes the absolute, unbridgeable "divorce" between Heaven and Hell. If even the farthest edge of Heaven is unbearable, how could a sinful soul endure the very presence of God himself? And so as the landscape of the grey town shows what the souls there have become, Lewis next constructs a Paradise to depict what God has prepared for those who choose him.

THE SIZE OF HEAVEN

When Lewis steps out of the bus, he finds himself in a new "kind" of space, so enormous it "made the Solar System itself seem an indoor affair. It gave me a feeling of freedom, but also of exposure, possibly of danger, which continued to accompany me through all that followed" (28). Lewis builds on this impression of vastness when he describes a vista that normal eyes on earth could not manage. On the horizon are forests, valleys stretching out in the distance, and mountains of impossible height, some evidently with cities on them, whereas the grey town was always flat. And yet these distant features are only the beginnings; deep Heaven itself is out of sight.

Heaven is not only unimaginably vast, as was the grey town; it also resembles the grey town in that it seems empty. But not for the same reason; the souls (now called Spirits) that have chosen Heaven have left the bus stop far behind in their journey up into the mountains toward the presence of God. Down in the grey town, people quarrel and move away from each other and so from the bus stop as well. The bus stop (God's grace shown in Christ) is the crucial and only connection between the two places; a place to avoid or the place to begin the journey toward Heaven.

Time in Heaven

The weather is perfect (finally, no rain), the air fresh, and yet once again Lewis finds himself in a place where time seems to stand still. But now dawn is about to break over the mountains rather than night. "The promise—or the threat—of sunrise rested immovably up there" (30). And the light once again allows Lewis to see the passengers, who are now uneasily beginning to move away from the bus into the countryside, in a new (excuse the pun) "light." They are transparent. "They were in fact ghosts: man-shaped stains on the brightness of that air. One could attend to them or ignore them at will as you do with the dirt on a window pane" (28).

The Density of Heaven

When Lewis finds he can look right through his fellow passengers, he also notices that the grass under their feet doesn't bend, nor are the drops of dew even disturbed. He experiments by attempting to pluck a daisy but the effort fails even though he tries so hard the skin comes off his hands. Next he tries to lift a small leaf but since it is heavier than a sack of coal he must abandon the effort. Even the blades of grass were sharp and, like everything else, as hard as diamonds. Exploring the countryside in any direction is a painful experience, and Lewis compares his pains to "those of the mermaid* in Hans Andersen" (32).

Dick, the Spirit who was sent to the Episcopal Ghost, reveals the meaning Lewis intended behind the strange conditions in Heaven. He invites the Ghost to come with him to the mountains, saying that although the trip will be painful at first, his feet would become harder. The reason for the pain? "Reality is harsh to the feet of shadows" (43). This is the key that unlocks the mystery of the "geography" in Heaven. Density and the weight it produces in objects represents the reality of life in Heaven.

The Direction to Heaven

The upward motion of the bus ride reflects the Biblical custom of referring to Heaven as "up" and Sheol/Hades or the underworld as "down." In reality, of course, people in Australia ("down under") pointing up to Heaven would, from our perspective, be pointing to a very different place. Let's agree that both "places" are part of the spirit world and that Lewis is using "up" and "down" to signify that a soul is moving toward God or away from Him. Thus, the invitation of Dick for the Episcopal Ghost to confess his heresy is expressed as a upward journey to the mountains on the horizon. The distance to them seems vast, but when the lizard of lust is killed by the Burning Angel so that it can become the stallion of true love, the spiritual progress of the Ghost becoming a Spirit is rapid indeed. The Spirit reminds Lewis of a shooting star as he climbs ever upward and finally disappears into the light above the mountains (101).

THE FUNCTION OF THE LANDSCAPE OF HEAVEN

Weight, hardness and density all serve to communicate the reality of Heaven. What Lewis is really saying is that as a soul moves closer to God it experiences more sharply the nature of God. Today God is chiefly described as a God of love, and rightly so, for He will reach out to any soul that will allow Him, but Lewis here means to emphasize the absolute holiness of God, without sacrificing His love. In His presence no sin whatsoever can be concealed. To make that attempt, to cling to self, is only to avoid the reality about oneself. God is a consuming fire (Heb 12:29) and to embrace that reality is painful but worthwhile, to say the least.

But how can Lewis communicate the terror that souls who dislike reality feel when they approach Reality Himself, when not a single soul experiences God directly in this book? The very landscape itself is the answer. It represents all the reality a Ghost can endure. Nearly everything is hard, dangerous, solid and painfully sharp. An insect or raindrop would go right through the tightly-stretched "bubbles" that the souls have become. Imagine what a lion could do. The Spirits who come to help them are terrifying in their solidity and appearance. And at the very end of the book, the rays of light that bring the dawn are like solid blocks of stone, causing Lewis to scream in terror and awake from his dream.

When the passengers arrive at their destination, they are little more than transparent bubbles on the landscape. Then Lewis's mind re-adjusts and he sees them for the people they actually are. Up to this point they have tried to avoid seeing themselves as God does, and that is why they have been in a place where the buildings, constructed by mere thought, can't even keep out the rain. And when Lewis asks the Episcopal Ghost where he's been living, he responds "Now that you mention it, I don't think we ever do give it a name" (40); another indication of their flight from reality.

Lewis waits until the end of his dream to reveal a surprising fact about the grey town. When Lewis wonders why Sarah Smith didn't accompany

Frank to the grey town, MacDonald smiles and plucks a blade of grass. They both kneel down (very painful for Lewis) and using the blade as a pointer, MacDonald shows Lewis a tiny crack in the soil. "I cannot be certain" he said, "that this *is* the crack ye came up through. But through a crack no bigger than that ye certainly came" (119).

Lewis is astonished, protesting "I saw an infinite Abyss. And cliffs towering up and up." Yes, MacDonald explains, but the trip was not just movement in an upward direction but the bus and its passengers were increasing in size. Hence, Lewis the author is saying, the spiritual progress the journey represents brought the passengers into greater contact with reality than the grey town could offer. But the "stretching" of the as-yet-unchanged souls meant they arrived as thin and transparent as soap becomes when mixed with water and blown up into bubbles.

The grey town appeared to be immense because people kept quarreling with each other and moving away somewhere else. But in reality, they were only collapsing into themselves, much like a star that collapses into itself and becomes a black hole in space, drawing everything around it into its intense gravitational field, until not even light can escape. "A dammed soul is nearly nothing: it is shrunk, shut up in itself." The amazing result: "All Hell is smaller than one pebble of your earthly world: but it is smaller than one atom of *this* world, the Real World" (120).

Summary of Part II

The "Geography" of *The Great Divorce*

Lewis has given vivid descriptions of the grey town and of Heaven, and yet they are not to be taken literally. "The transmortal conditions are solely an imaginative supposal: they are not even a guess or a speculation at what may actually await us. The last thing I wish is to arouse factual curiosity about the details of the after-world" (11). Lewis knew that every depiction of the spirit world would fall short of the truth, and to imply otherwise would be misleading. "No, I don't wish I knew Heaven was like the picture in my *Great Divorce*, because, if we knew that, we should know it was no better" (CLIII, "To Mrs Johnson," August 7, 1956; 778).

And so MacDonald warns him (and anyone who would try) in their final conversation that should Lewis share his dream with the world, he should

> Make it plain that it was but a dream. See ye make it very plain. Give no poor fool the pretext to think ye are claiming knowledge of what no mortal knows. I'll have no Swedenborges and no Vale Owens* among my children.
>
> God forbid, Sir, said I, trying to look very wise.
>
> He *has* forbidden it. That's what I'm telling ye.

Lewis was curious about the spirit world, as most Christians are, but when he searched the Scriptures, he was forced to conclude that God does not wish to reveal details about spiritual landscapes. "The Bible seems scrupulously to avoid any *descriptions* of the other world, or worlds, except in terms of parable or allegory" (CLIII, "To Vera Gebbert," October 16, 1960; 1198).

Still, he was open to the possibility that some humans might possess traces of faculties that were much stronger before the fall, or are waiting to come into full strength after the resurrection, and that these faculties could bring hints of the spirit world. But only hints. "...If more knowledge is to come, it must be the wordless & thoughtless knowledge of the mystic: not the celestial statistics of Swedenborg, the Lemurian history of Steiner, or the demonology of the Platonists" (CLI, "To Cecil Harwood," October 28, 1926; 671) .

And yet the "geography" does have a significance; Lewis constructed his places so that they would have a theological message. The grey town serves double duty, depicting what the life of the soul is like when souls are avoiding reality and truth, and therefore God himself. Intellectual life and spiritual growth have died, and the image of God in others only leads to quarrels and self-isolation. Yet the place also reflects to a small degree the reality that cannot be fully avoided, since God is everywhere. The rain continues to fall, giving the lie to the hope that the houses (facades) they erect just by thinking of them are real enough to protect them from the danger to come.

Leaving the grey town, the riders on the bus found themselves flying over an Abyss, the same chasm that separated the Rich Man from Lazarus in the parable of Jesus recorded by Luke. This "infinite" (120) Abyss that no human can bridge underscores the leading theme of the book and so assists Lewis as he combats the "perennial" attempt to marry Heaven and Hell (9). And yet, sincere repentance will bring Heaven's help; the Abyss can be crossed and Heaven reached by divine grace. Lewis repeatedly stresses this promise of salvation being near at hand in the conversations between the Ghosts and the Spirits. The exchange between the self-conscious Ghost and a Spirit is typical. When she asks about the purpose of life, the Spirit sent to her replies, "For infinite happiness. You can step out into it at any moment" (61).

And what about the sharp blades of grass ("Horrible spikes!" 60) and the iron-hard flower stalks? The uncomfortable surroundings of Heaven are not the will of God, any more than permanent residence in the grey town. Heaven stands ready to help the Ghosts "thicken up" so that the surroundings will indeed become a Paradise. Since too much reality for newly-arrived passengers would be fatal, human Spirits come to help the Ghosts, not God himself. One angel also comes, but his brightness and heat are nearly unbearable.

All the surroundings, in stark contrast to the mean streets below, call out to the Ghosts in their beauty and declare the wisdom of their Creator. When Ikey attempts to take a golden apple back down to the grey town, a waterfall is transformed to reveal a bright angel, standing as if crucified, pouring over the rocks with loud joy. He speaks to Ikey and tells him to abandon his hopeless quest. Instead, he should stay so that in time he will be able to eat the golden apples. "The very leaves and blades of grass in the wood will delight to teach you" (51). Ikey ignores Heaven's advice, but Lewis understands that the life of Christ who was crucified now permeates the spirit world in the place He has prepared for mankind, and he desires souls to be comfortable in that new environment.

In the final analysis, to accept Heaven is the same, for Lewis, as accepting reality. The only other choice is to create one's own reality, and that path leads to insanity and the death of the soul. This difference between Hell and

Heaven comes to Lewis with a rebuke when he asks his tour guide if they are correct who believe Hell and Heaven are only states of mind. "Hush...Do not blaspheme," MacDonald cautions him.

> Hell is a state of mind—ye never said a truer word. And every state of mind, left to itself, every shutting up of the creature within the dungeon of its own mind—is, in the end, Hell. But Heaven is not a state of mind. Heaven is reality itself. All that is fully real is Heavenly. For all that can be shaken will be shaken and only the unshakeable remains (68. Compare the words of Milton: "The mind is its own place, and in itself, Can make a Heaven of Hell, a Hell of Heaven." *Paradise Lost*, Ch. 1.).

How then does a state of mind compare with reality? It can't, and once a person understands this, he will abandon any attempt to marry Heaven and Hell and Lewis will have accomplished what he set out to do in this book. Lewis uses hyperbole to get across this crucial point: MacDonald points to a butterfly and tells Lewis "If it swallowed all Hell, Hell would not be big enough to do it any harm or to have any taste" (120).

MacDonald next tells Lewis that "If all Hell's miseries together entered the consciousness of yon wee yellow bird on the bough there, they would be swallowed up without trace, as if one drop of ink had been dropped into that Great Ocean to which your terrestrial Pacific itself is only a molecule" (120). Lewis begins to grasp the idea; those in Hell are in flight from reality (portrayed by the solid and heavy landscape, animals and Spirits in Paradise) and there is no room for reality there.

Is it all hopeless, then? Could the bird make itself smaller, like Alice* did? No, says MacDonald, even if it could shrink itself in size, it still wouldn't be small enough. But there is One who was able to enter Hell, and that is Jesus. The reason he could go there is because "Only the Greatest of all can make Himself small enough to enter Hell. For the higher a thing is, the lower it can descend... Only One has descended into Hell" (121).

So yes, there is hope. Between the crucifixion and the resurrection, Christ did descend into Hell, or better yet, Hades, a region of Hell or, depending on the soul, of Heaven. What he accomplished there and its implications for all of humanity will now be explained in Part III.

PART III

The Theology of *The Great Divorce*

Drawn from the new age and antiquity,
>This realm of saints, whose joy no dangers mar,
>Gazed on one sign in love and unity.

To charity their faces sweetly woo,
>Made beauteous in our Maker's light and smile,
>And gracious dignity their gestures show.
>>(*Paradise*, Canto xxxi. 25-27; 49-51: 328.)

C. S. Lewis Goes to Heaven

CHAPTER 1

The Descent of Christ

Lewis, as Dante before him, didn't actually describe the descent of Christ into Hades, but everything in their respective works assumes and depends upon this event. The premise for both is that Christ entered Hades, took authority over the place, and now "tours" are possible, at least in fiction. Lewis also follows Dante in stressing that the souls who "belong" to Christ as a result of their encounter with him in Hades do not immediately see God himself. Much spiritual growth is necessary first. Dante portrays ten ascending levels of Heaven, while Lewis describes mountains in the distance that rise so high that "Deep Heaven" is far out of sight for those who have just arrived on the bus.

CHRIST'S DESCENT TO HADES

In his sermon on the Day of Pentecost, Peter told his listeners that the coming of the Holy Spirit was evidence that Jesus had been raised from the dead. After visiting and teaching his disciples for forty days (Acts 1:3), he ascended into Heaven where he received the Spirit from the Father and sent Him into the world (Acts 2:33). But what happened between the crucifixion and the resurrection of Jesus? Understanding this brief period of time is the key to Lewis' understanding of Purgatory.

In the same sermon, Peter quotes the words of David who long ago expressed his hope that God would not allow his body to experience decay, nor abandon his soul in Hades. Since he did die and his body underwent decay, Peter explains that David's prophetic words actually were fulfilled in the life of Jesus. "He was not abandoned to Hades, nor did his flesh experience corruption" (Acts 2:25-31 DC; a fulfillment of Psa 16:10).

Thus Jesus experienced death as a human being, but since he was sinless, he was not subject to death long enough for his body to decay nor was his soul confined to Hades. His resurrection and appearance to more than five hundred people is proof of this victory over death and Hades. In the last book of the New Testament, he identifies himself to John on the island of Patmos with the words "I was dead, and see, I am alive forever and ever; and I have the keys of Death and of Hades" (Rev 1:18 NRSV.) By "keys" he meant that he, not death, had control over his body, and that his soul could not be confined to Sheol. But what does his personal victory mean to humanity?

THE DESCENT IN CHURCH TRADITION

This deliverance of souls by Christ has long been a traditional belief of the Christian church, and in his correspondence, Lewis explained how it became a part of his own theology.

> What is v. much more important is that the ancients may have been right. The N.T. always speaks of Christ not as one who taught, or demonstrated, the possibility of a glorious after life but as one who first created that possibility—the Pioneer, the First Fruits, the Man who forced the door. This of course links up with Peter 1:III 20 about preaching to the spirits in prison and explains why Our Lord 'descended into Hell' (= *Sheol* or Hades). It looks v. much as if, till His resurrection, the fate of the dead actually *was* a shadowy half-life—mere ghosthood. The medieval authors delighted to picture what they called 'the harrowing of Hell', Christ descending and knocking on those eternal doors and bringing out those whom He chose. I believe in something like this. It wd. explain how what Christ did can save those who lived long before the Incarnation. (CLIII, "To Audrey Sutherland," April 28, 1960; 1148)

In a remarkable Easter poem from his own pen, Lewis vividly described this part of Christ's redemptive work.

> Loudly roaring from the regions
> Where no sunbeam e'er was shed,
> Rise and dance, ye ransomed legions
> Of the cold and countless dead!
> Gates of adamant are broken,
> Words of conquering power are spoken
> Through the God who died and bled:
> > Hell lies vacant, spoiled and cheated,
> > By the Lord of life defeated.

(CLIII, "To Francis Turner," June 10, 1958; 956). (One fourth of poem.)

Dante also celebrated the same event. When Dante follows his tour guide Virgil into the First Circle on the edge of the actual pit of Hell, they come to Limbo, where the unbaptized and the virtuous pagans have a "suspended" existence. They are excluded from the bliss of God's presence since they did not pay the proper tributes to God, but experience no torment, since they did not sin. Dante is deeply touched by their condition, and asks if any pre-Christians did leave Hell. Dante replies that he had not been in Hades very long ("When I was newly in this state") when he beheld an awesome conqueror appear and bring salvation to those in Hades. Using A. D. 33 as the traditional date of the crucifixion, Virgil had been dead for fifty-two years. Here are Dante's question and Virgil's answer:

> "Tell me, sir–tell me, Master," I began
> (In hope some fresh assurance to be gleaning
> Of our sin-conquering Faith), "did any man
>
> By his self-merit, or on another leaning,
> Ever fare forth from hence and come to be
> Among the blest?" He took my hidden meaning.
>
> "When I was newly in this state," said he,
> "I saw One come in majesty and awe,
> And on His head were crowns of victory.
>
> Our great first father's spirit He did withdraw,
> And righteous Abel, Noah who built the ark,
> Moses who gave and who obeyed the Law,
>
> King David, Abraham the Patriarch,
> Israel with his father and generation,
> Rachel, for whom he did such deeds of mark,
>
> With many another of His chosen nation;
> These did He bless; and know, that ere that day
> No human soul had ever seen salvation."
> (Hell, Canto IV: 46-63, pp. 92-3.)

Dante, like Lewis, based his theology upon the traditions of the church, and the Scriptures as he understood them. And both of them concluded that there was solid support in both Bible and tradition for the life of Christ to include the personal conquest of Hades. And the implications for believers are profound. Salvation in Christ will, when complete, include the whole person; body and soul. Wherever the body is—grave, tomb, dust, or any place—it will be raised up. And wherever the soul that has chosen God exists after death—Sheol, Hades, the Pit, Paradise—it will be reunited with the risen body.

Biblical Support for Christ's Descent

Before the Descent

The Christian hope that Jesus will someday raise the dead and bring the souls from the spirit world to be reunited with their resurrected bodies rests upon the words of Jesus himself. In the Gospel of John, he promises his disciples "Because I live, you shall live also" (John 14:19). And his description of his return to earth includes the promise that at his command, the angels will gather the "elect" from the farthest extents of the spirit world, and from the "ends of the earth" (Mark 13:27; see also Rev 20:13 where Hades, the place for souls, gives up the dead so they can be judged). So then, his keys or authority over death and Hades include all of humanity; both bodies and souls, wherever those souls might be in the spirit world and wherever those bodies might be in the natural world.

Near the end of his earthly life, Jesus shared with his disciples what he was about to do, including his own death by crucifixion and resurrection. But I believe some of what he said pertains to his activity in the spirit world after the crucifixion. John alone has preserved these traditions; perhaps his openness to and understanding of these deeper truths partly explain why John was the "beloved" disciple of Jesus.

In the first passage, Jesus uses the metaphor of sheep and shepherd to describe himself and his followers.

> "Truly, truly, I say to you, he who does not enter the sheepfold by the door but climbs in by another way, that man is a thief and a robber; [2] but he who enters by the door is the shepherd of the sheep"... [6] This figure Jesus used with them, but they did not understand what he was saying to them. [7] So Jesus again said to them, "Truly, truly, I say to you, I am the door of the sheep. [8] All who came before me are thieves and robbers; but the sheep did not heed them... I am the door... I am the good shepherd" (John 10:1-2, 6-9, 11).

Here Jesus claims to be the only shepherd of humanity who can lead them to salvation, and by "sheep" Jesus meant his own people who were the focus of his ministry (for the most part), as shown in his instructions to his disciples: [5] These twelve Jesus sent out after instructing them, saying, "Go nowhere among the Gentiles, and enter no town of the Samaritans; [6] but go rather to the lost sheep of the house of Israel" (Matt 10:5-6).

But in the same chapter, Jesus reveals that he will become the leader of other "sheep," which I take to mean people groups. [16] "And I have other sheep, that are not of this fold; I must bring them also, and they will heed my voice. So there shall be one flock, one shepherd" (John 10:16). Once again, a universal aspect is hinted at. Since Jesus is about to die, not many more living people will hear his voice. But dead people are just as important to God, and this remarkable promise Jesus made to his disciples convinced Lewis that those "sheep" would also hear the message of salvation.

The next chapter in John confirms the authority of Jesus over death (of the body) and Hades. Lazarus the friend of Jesus is sick. Jesus waits until he is dead, and then informs his disciples that he is going to Lazarus and asks them to come with him. The response of Thomas suggests that he understood the words of Jesus concerning his other sheep to mean that Jesus will reach those other sheep by dying and entering the spirit world.

> [13] Now Jesus had spoken of his death, but they thought that he was speaking of literal sleep. [14] Then Jesus therefore said to them plainly, "Lazarus is dead, [15] and I am glad for your sakes that I was not there, so that you may believe; but let us go to him." [16] Thomas therefore, who is called Didymus, said to his fellow disciples, "Let us also go, that we may die with him" (John 11:13-16 NRSV).

When Jesus finally arrived at the house of Lazarus, he was met by his grief-stricken sisters, Martha first and then Mary. By this time, Lazarus had been dead for four days. The rabbis believed that after three days the soul permanently left the body, so whether or not this is actually true, Jesus delayed his coming so that there would be no doubt in anyone's mind that Lazarus was truly dead and his soul departed to Hades. Martha believed that Lazarus would rise "on the last day" (John 11:24), but now she learned that Jesus himself would be the one who would raise the dead.

As Jesus would soon demonstrate, he did not need to die and descend to Hades to revive the body of Lazarus and bring back his soul from Hades, The raising of Lazarus was the proof that he had authority of death and Hades. But Jesus also understood that his death would atone for sin and would also enable him to be (potentially) the shepherd for all humanity, although many will reject him if Lewis is correct.

John depicts this expectation of Jesus when he reports that "some Greeks" who had come for the Passover wanted to meet with Jesus. Instead of receiving them or sending them away, Jesus instead states that the time has come for him to die. But then he adds "And I, when I am lifted up from the earth, will draw all men to myself.' [3] He said this to show by what death he was to die" (John 12:32-33).

This astonishing prediction (promise?) comes in the form of a typical, two-part conditional statement; in this case, a future condition. The "if" clause states what may in the future take place, and the "then" clause gives the result that will occur if that future event does occur. In other words, the relationship between the two clauses is that the death of Jesus will make possible the result of all humanity coming to Jesus.

Unfortunately, John only comments on the conditional clause, telling his readers that the words of Jesus show he knew beforehand how he would die. In this way the early church could tell its detractors that the crucifixion was not a tragic end to the life of Jesus but that Jesus chose to die on the cross to fulfill God's plan that made redemption possible.

But the second clause is just as important, though Jesus does not explain *how* his death will result in him "drawing" (the Greek verb also means to "drag," or "pull") all humanity to himself. Nor does the passage reveal *where* this will occur, *when* all humanity will be gathered together to him, or even *why* he will do this. But it is clear that the crucifixion will set into motion a series of events that will ultimately involve all of humanity, dead and alive.

Jesus revealed still more to his disciples when he ate the Passover with them just before his betrayal and arrest. "In my Father's house are many rooms; if it were not so, would I have told you that I go to prepare a place for you?" (John 14:2). The Parable of the Rich Man and Lazarus described two of those places; now Jesus reveals that yet another place will be constructed. Is it so unreasonable to conclude that the other sheep (souls) that Jesus planned to reach were in the "many" rooms or dwelling places, and would be taken from them and brought into his new "environment"?

AFTER THE DESCENT

After Jesus ascended into Heaven, the early church began to reflect upon his words to them. Three of the most important Biblical passages that describe the activity of Christ in Hades are Eph 4:8-11, 1 Pet 3:18-20, and 1 Pet 4:6.

> Eph 4:8-11 [8]Therefore it is said, "When he ascended on high he led a host of captives; and he gave gifts to men." [9](In saying, "He ascended," what does it mean but that he had also descended into the lower parts of the earth? [10]He who descended is he who ascended far above all the heavens, so that he might fill all things.) [11] And his gifts were that some should be apostles, some prophets, some evangelists, some pastors and teachers...

> 1 Pet 3:18-20 [18]For Christ also suffered for sins once for all, the righteous for the unrighteous, in order to bring you to God. He was put to death in the flesh, but made alive in the spirit, [19]in which also he went and made a proclamation to the spirits in prison, [20]who in former times did not obey, when God waited patiently in the days of Noah, during the building of the ark, in which a few, that is, eight persons, were saved through water. (NRSV)

1 Peter 4:6 For this is why the gospel was preached even to the dead, that though judged in the flesh like men, they might live in the spirit like God.

Near the end of *The Great Divorce*, Lewis directly refers to the second passage when he has MacDonald say "there is no spirit in prison to whom He did not preach" (121). A minor correction is in order. Most scholars agree "spirits in prison" refers not to human souls as Lewis thought but to the lustful angels that came down in Noah's time, married human women, taught mankind many dangerous skills, and so corrupted the world that God wiped it out by a flood (Gen 6:1-7, and several intertestamental Jewish sources such as I Enoch). Peter returns to this theme in his second epistle, adding that the angels are imprisoned in Tartarus, the lowest section of Hades in ancient mythology (2 Pet 2:4; see also Jude 6). Peter likely meant that Christ told them that their attempts to corrupt the human race by intermarriage and so prevent the birth of the promised redeemer had failed.

At any rate, the third passage does refer to human souls. Peter clearly states that Jesus went to Hades to proclaim the gospel to deceased humans. Some modern translations read "... even to those who are *now* dead" but the word "now" is not in the Greek text. Combining all the texts, Christ's journey to Hades took Him first to the lowest part where the angels were and are still imprisoned. Then, moving "upward" and "leading captivity captive", he freed the human souls from Hades who were willing to go with him and brought them into Paradise, the place he prepared for them.

Next, the resurrection of his body and the exit from Hades of his soul brought Jesus once again into time and space of this world. Luke records that Jesus met with this disciples for a period of forty days, teaching them about the kingdom of God, and even eating with them (Acts 1:3). Then he ascended into Heaven as they watched, took his place at the right hand of God, and finally sent the Holy Spirit on the day of Pentecost, the event that gave birth to the church and equipped it with the ministries of apostle, prophet, evangelist, pastor and teacher (Eph 4:8-11).

When Paul describes Christ's descent in Eph 4:9-10, he writes "when he ascended... he led a host of captives". In other words, some souls did leave the underworld and ascend with Christ, probably to Paradise, or the "outskirts" of Heaven; the setting in which Lewis places most of *The Great Divorce*. But who left with Christ? Only those who wanted to, who were willing to embrace Truth Himself, Lewis would answer. Perhaps Jesus was speaking to the Pharisees about his descent, before it happened in time, but already known in the eternal present, when He told them that Abraham, whom they respected so highly, not only wanted to know about Christ, but had indeed seen "my day", and rejoiced at what he saw (John 8:56).

And, I might add, those who went with Christ to Heaven shall again accompany him when he returns. As Paul reminds the Thessalonians, "God will bring with Jesus those who have fallen asleep (died) in him" (1 Thess 4:14). Thus there is biblical support, both direct and indirect, for the historical Christian belief in the descent of Christ to the underworld and for some of the dead leaving their chambers in Hades and ascending with Christ to Heaven.

CHAPTER 2

The Choice and the Change

The ever-curious Lewis posed all manner of questions to his guide (as did Dante before him), but MacDonald reins in his pupil and directs him to the crux of the matter: the choice that lies before every human and which must be made. "Ye cannot fully understand the relations of choice and Time till you are beyond both. And ye were not brought here to study such curiosities. What concerns you is the nature of the choice itself: and that ye can watch them making" (69). Now for a closer look.

THE UNIVERSAL AND UNAVOIDABLE CHOICE

As Lewis reflected upon the theological views people hold, he identified what he considered to be a "disastrous error"; namely, "the belief that reality never presents us with an absolutely unavoidable "either-or"" (9). A huge amount of unstated theology lies behind this view, but to simplify matters, I'll point out a few essential truths that led Lewis to this conclusion.

First, Lewis is guided here by the Biblical theology that God created humanity and wishes to enjoy fellowship with mankind. Since he has given each person a will separate from his own, every human must choose or reject God, and that choice will lead either to Heaven or Hell. No one is excluded. Atheists will learn there is a God, and people of all religions or none at all will also choose. There simply is no escape. God is humanity's source, sustaining power, destination, and the ultimate reality.

Lewis also agrees with the New Testament teaching that the right choice will lead not just to "God" in some general, non-specific sense, but to Jesus, who claimed "I am the way... no one comes to the Father except through me" (John 14:6 NRSV). In this way, Biblical statements that seem quite simplistic can be reconciled with the complexity of human existence. To speak of all humanity as either sheep or goats (Matt 25:31-46), or to claim as Jesus did that everyone would be drawn toward him seems to be at odds with the reality that people follow many religions, or none at all, that millions have never even heard of

Christ, and that people are in countless stages of spiritual development, from little if any to advanced spirituality. But if, in this life or after death, everyone will, (indeed, must) encounter Christ, the ultimate source of truth and life, and the ultimate reality, then at the end of all things, only be two options will remain.

THE FINAL CHOICE

This universal and unavoidable choice is better understood as a series of choices; perhaps thousands of choices in a typical human life, but always leading up to a final choice. Lewis does not mean in this context all choices, such as "what will I wear today," or "shall I go for a walk after dinner," but *moral* choices. These choices affect the soul, and over time a person becomes more and more shaped by them. "...Every time you make a choice you are turning the central part of you... either into a Heavenly creature or into a Hellish creature" (MC: 72).

Since each moral choice shapes the soul, there are limitations to the freedom to choose. "But though freedom is real it is not infinite. Every choice reduces a little ones (sic) freedom to choose the next time. There therefore becomes a time when the creature is fully *built*, irrevocably attached either to God or to itself. This irrevocableness is what we call Heaven or Hell" (CLII:"To Joyce Pearce," July 20, 1943, p. 585). Only God knows when a creature is fully "built", when no more choices are possible. Nor did Lewis view physical death as the time of final choice. Most people are not capable of any rational choices at the time of death. Others may have permanently chosen their course long before death; consider those who preferred martyrdom over denying their Savior. And still others, perhaps most of humanity, are still works in progress at the time of death.

IS LEWIS GIVING HUMANITY A SECOND CHANCE?

The main objection to the concept of souls choosing Heaven or Hell after death is that it seems to offer the possibility of salvation after death. Why should people get a "second chance" if they have rejected God when they had a "first chance" during their earthly life? Fair question. But the Protestants who object to a "second chance" (and most Protestants do) also believe that salvation only comes through Jesus. If so, then most people who have ever lived never even had a first choice. Even now, two thousand years after the resurrection, there are still millions who have never heard of Jesus.

Now what is so interesting about the approach Lewis takes is that everyone has the chance to choose or reject Jesus, and yet no one can avoid that choice. Every person within or outside of Christianity chooses, or rejects, the good and the upright as he is able to understand it. One might say that Lewis has found the "lowest common denominator" since everyone makes moral choices, no matter when or where they live or lived. And when you get right down to it, no one, even the most enlightened believer, is able to do any more than that. What matters above all is the desire to know and obey the truth, and to do what is right.

But what of salvation in Christ and Christ alone? Lewis certainly did not think that moral choices were sufficient for salvation. New life comes only from Christ. So then, the reality is the series of choices every human makes, not a first or second chance. A real "second chance" is impossible; as Lewis observes, it would be "a new earthly life in which you cd. attempt afresh all the problems you failed at in the present one (as in religions of Re-Incarnation)." But Purgatory, as Lewis understands it, is "a process by which the work of redemption continues, and first perhaps begins to be noticeable after death" (CLIII, "To Mrs Johnson," November 8, 1952; 245).

Does the possibility of everyone encountering Christ then rob the Gospel of its urgency, as many suppose? No. The sooner a person hears, the more opportunities there are for making good moral choices, for developing a deep relationship with God, and for bringing a Christian witness to the world. And the Bible does promise rewards for the deeds done in the body (1 Cor 3:10-15).

TIME AND BEYOND TIME

By now it's clear that both Dante and Lewis believed that souls would experience time differently in the spirit world than they did while alive on earth. Dante described salvation coming to Adam, Noah, and many others; both Israelites and those who lived before Israel became a nation. And Lewis writes, "All moments... are... present in the moment of His descending" (121). How can this be when Christ descended into Hades thousands of years after Adam lived and died?

First, Lewis knew that this question will never be answered if Christian theology assumes that God's existence is limited to time and space as we experience them.

> Almost certainly God is not in Time. His life does not consist of moments following one another. If a million people are praying to Him at ten-thirty tonight, He need not listen to them all in that one little snippet which we call ten-thirty. Ten-thirty—and every other moment from the beginning of the world—is always the Present for Him... If you picture Time as a straight line along which we have to travel, then you must picture God as the whole page on which the line is drawn. We come to the parts of the line one by one; we have to leave A behind

before we get to B, and cannot reach C until we leave B behind. God, from above or outside or all round, contains the whole line, and sees it all (MC: 131-132).

Lewis next explores this understanding of God and concludes that when a person acts, God sees that action in his eternal present. "…if God *foresaw* our acts, it would be very hard to understand how we could be free not to do them" (MC 133). This viewpoint sheds light on the betrayal of Judas. That betrayal was prophesied in the Old Testament (Psa 41:9), but Judas was not forced to betray Jesus with a kiss in order to fulfill the prophecy. Rather, Lewis would say, God (in his eternal present) saw Judas freely choose to betray Jesus. Since all of time is present to God, he was able in that eternal present to inspire David to speak of it in the Psalms. From our perspective within time, we marvel at the fulfillment of a prophecy given one thousand years beforehand, and so we speak of *pre*destination and *fore*knowledge. But all time is in the present tense for God.

Lewis also explains that when God looks at humanity, he does not see billions of separate individuals from his perspective both in and above or outside time.

> If you could see humanity spread out in time, as God sees it, it would not look like a lot of separate things dotted about. It would look like one single growing thing–rather like a very complicated tree. Every individual would appear connected with every other. And not only that. Individuals are not really separate from God any more than from one another. Every man, woman, and child all over the world is feeling and breathing at this moment only because God, so to speak, is "keeping him going" (MC: 141).

Next, Lewis brings Jesus into this image of corporate humanity stretched out through time, from today and back to Adam and Eve. When the Christ who has been sustaining all creation becomes man, the change begins.

> From that point the effect spreads through all mankind. It makes a difference to people who lived before Christ as well as to people who lived after Him. It makes a difference to people who have never heard of Him. It is like dropping into a glass of water one drop of something which gives a new taste or a new colour to the whole lot… The business of becoming a son of God, of being turned from a created thing into a begotten thing, of passing over from the temporary biological life into timeless "spiritual" life, has been done for us. Humanity is already "saved" in principle. We individuals have to appropriate that salvation… If we will only lay ourselves open to the one Man in whom it was fully present… He will do it in us and for us (MC 141).

These are powerful assertions with far-reaching implications for the entire human race. But Lewis did not explain in *Mere Christianity* how this "effect spreads through all mankind." And that is why *The Great Divorce* is so important. The solution given through MacDonald is to leave this world of space and time, and take a bus ride to the timeless spirit world where all souls arrive at the "same time," so to speak, when death occurs. There, Christ who descended to Hades between his death on the cross and his resurrection offers salvation to everyone who has ever lived and ever will live. Lewis mentioned this view in his correspondence, when he interpreted the 1 Pet 4 passage (the Gospel preached to the dead): "that would be outside time, and include those who died long after Him as well as those who died before He was born as Man" (CLIII, "To Mary Van Deusen," January 31, 1952; 163).

This theology gives new depth to many biblical passages. For example, the promise God made to Abraham: "And by your descendents shall *all* the nations of the earth bless themselves, because you have obeyed my voice" (Gen 22:18). Or consider the fulfillment of this promise when John saw around the throne of God people "from *every* nation, from all tribes and peoples and tongues" (Rev 7:9). Only Christ's timeless activity in Hades that gives everyone a chance to accept or reject his salvation makes these passages literally possible.

But do the souls in Hades there still experience time as they did on earth, or do they experience time as God does? The Bible does not provide the answer, but Lewis offers a plausible view when writing to his fictional correspondent, Malcolm, who (Lewis pretends) holds view that the dead are no longer in time.

> How do you know they are not? I certainly believe that to be God is to enjoy an infinite present, where nothing has yet passed away and nothing is still to come. Does it follow that we can say the same of saints and angels? Or at any rate exactly the same? The dead might experience a time which was not quite so linear as ours—it might, so to speak, have thickness as well as length. Already in this life we get some thickness whenever we learn to attend to more than one thing at once. One can suppose this increased to any extent, so that though, for them as for us, the present is always becoming the past, yet each present contains unimaginably more than ours (LTM: 109-110).

Sheldon Vanauken published a few letters of Lewis in his book *A Severe Mercy*, and this very topic appears in that correspondence.

> What you say about time is what I've long thought. It is inadequate to, and partially transcended by, v. simple experiences. E.g. *when* do we hear a musical air? Until the last note is sounded it is incomplete; as soon as that sounds it's already over. And I'm pretty sure eternal life

doesn't mean this width-less line of moments endlessly prolonged (as if by prolongation it cd. 'catch up with' that wh. it so obviously cd. never hold) but getting off that line onto its plane or even the solid. (CLIII, "To Sheldon Vanauken," June 5, 1955; 616.)

In yet another letter, Lewis evoked the landscape of Paradise as he described it in *The Great Divorce*. "I suppose this is partly due to the nature of time—there being no real *present*, every moment already past however quickly you try to grab it. How rich we shall be when we get off this single railway-line into the rich green country left and right (CLIII, "To Mary Van Duesen," February 5, 1956; 701).

This spectrum of time Lewis is proposing may not be so strange after all. Between the experience of time as a succession of moments, and, at the other end of the spectrum, God's experience of all time as present, there may be points in between ("rich green country"), where time is still experienced, but more of it at the same time. (Obviously some new terminology is needed.) Logic suggests that souls in Hades would need to experience the passing of time in some manner, so that they can still choose between Heaven and Hell and can experience the changes that result from those choices. Sayers agrees: "Hell and Heaven are eternal states, but the life of Purgatory, like that of earth, is a temporal process, and time is of the very essence. ... Dallying is a postponement of beatitude; even, in a sense, a robbery of God, who looks for the home-coming of His own" (*Purgatory*: 20. Lewis also thought of souls arriving in Heaven as a "home-coming." His original title for *The Great Divorce* was "*Who Goes Home?*"). But the important thing in all of this speculation is that Christ himself, once he left the earth by death and returned to the spirit world, was not limited by time as he was while in his physical body.

But is there scriptural support for everyone who has ever lived having the opportunity to encounter Christ when he left space and time and "descended" into Hades? The passages that speak most directly to this question are found in the book of Hebrews. There, in Chapter 11, the unknown author lists several persons mentioned in the Old Testament, beginning with Abel, the son of Adam and Eve. Perhaps this is where Dante got the idea for his list of people who were redeemed from Hades, beginning with Adam.

Although all of these people, including an unnamed multitude from the times between the Old and New Testaments, pleased God because of their faith, they lived before Jesus was born and so their full salvation was not possible. "All these, though they were commended for their faith, did not receive what was promised, since God had provided something better so that they would not, apart from us, *be made perfect*" (Heb 11:39-40 NRSV).

In the next chapter, the writer continues to persuade the readers to remain faithful to Christ. If they return to their former lives under the Law of Moses because they are being persecuted (Heb 12:3), they will no longer have salvation in Christ. Instead, they need to understand their new position in God's redemption: "You have come to Mount Zion and to the city of the living God, the Heavenly Jerusalem... and to the spirits of the righteous *made perfect*" (Heb 12: 22-23 NRSV).

The implications are clear: from the time of Adam on, salvation of the soul in its fullest expression, the removal of all sins from the soul, was not possible. But now that Christ has died, descended, conquered Hades, and opened Paradise, those who lived and died before Christ have now been brought to perfection after death, and, as a "cloud of witnesses," watch (and cheer for) those who are now alive and are running the race of life (Heb 12:1-2).

I believe it's significant that the author of Hebrews referred to the perfected souls of the various people from Old Testament times who pleased God by their faith as "spirits" rather than souls. There is a symmetry here between our bodies and our souls. Paul tells us that our physical bodies will raised up as spiritual bodies (1 Cor 15:44). Likewise, our souls begin the transition to spirits when we are born again and finally become pure spirit when fully sanctified. Perhaps this very text in Hebrews 12:23 inspired Lewis to refer to the (sanctified) citizens of Heaven who came to meet the ghosts as "Spirits."

WILL ALL BE SAVED?

When MacDonald tells Lewis that Christ preached to every soul in "prison," Lewis begins to ponder the implications. "In your own books, Sir," said I, "you were a Universalist. You talked as if all men would be saved. And St. Paul too" (121). But MacDonald avoids the label, and tells Lewis that the answer to the question "who will be saved?" is beyond human knowledge.

> Ye can know nothing of the end of all things, or nothing expressible in those terms. It may be, as the Lord said to the Lady Julian, that all will be well, and all will be well, and all manner of things will be well. But it's ill talking of such questions... all answers deceive. If ye put the question from within Time and are asking about possibilities, the answer is certain. The choice of ways is before you. Neither is closed. Any man may choose eternal death. Those who choose it will have it (121-122).

MacDonald (that is, Lewis through MacDonald) goes on to explain that in this life, the only way to view the freedom of each human to choose Heaven or Hell is through the lens of time. When we try to step outside of time to understand eternal reality, we lose freedom. By this Lewis means that if we interpret the eternal purposes of God to mean that everyone will ultimately be saved, then the freedom of a person to choose Hell is lost. On the other hand, if some are predestined to be saved and the rest lost, then the freedom to choose Heaven is sacrificed.

In this final conversation with MacDonald, which included a vision of a chessboard, Lewis set forth the boundaries of his theology. There were many influences upon Lewis during his life, but of particular importance were his tutor Kirkpatrick, and his tour guide, MacDonald. How interesting that the person who was perhaps the most important intellectual influence upon Lewis was an atheist and the person who was perhaps the most important spiritual influence had the reputation of being a Universalist.

Lewis obviously left his time as an atheist behind, but what about the tug of MacDonald's influence? Will all be saved? Shouldn't all be saved? Lewis certainly courted the idea. He referred to the writings of both St. Paul and Julian of Norwich that could be interpreted as supporting Universalism. Lewis did not cite any passages from Paul's epistles, but perhaps he was thinking of 1 Timothy 4:10, a passage that seems to lean toward universalism: "For to this end we toil and strive, because we have our hope set on the living God, who is the Savior of all men, especially of those who believe."

MacDonald (Lewis) referred to Lady Julian in the quotation just above, and she is mentioned several other times in his writings. Lewis seems to regard her as someone who did receive valid revelations, and he obviously found her love and devotion to Christ inspiring. "I love Dame Julian" he declared. (CLIII, "To Father Peter Milward SJ," February 2, 1955; 558). Would she have the answer to the question of universalism?

Her enigmatic answer is quoted above: "all will be well". She claimed that Jesus revealed to her that "Sin is necessary, but all shall be well, and all shall be well, and all manner of things shall be well." (Julian: 102) But do these words mean every human being from Adam on will be saved? And what of fallen angels? More than this was not revealed to her; except that God would perform a "Grand Deed" at the end of time. Jesus also told her that God will not reveal to any person beforehand what that act will be.

In a letter to his brother Warren, Lewis shows how much he was intrigued, and frustrated, by what he found in the writings of Lady Julian.

> Very odd too is her doctrine of "the Grand Deed." Christ tells her again and again "All shall be well, and all will be well, and all manner of thing will be well." She asks how it can be well, since some are damned. He replied that all that is true, but the secret grand deed will make even that "very well". "With you this is impossible, but not with me."
>
> My mood changes about this. Sometimes it seems mere drivel–to invent a necessarily inconceivable grand deed which makes everything quite different while leaving it exactly the same. But then at other times

it has the unanswerable, illogical convincingness of things heard in a dream and appeals to what is one of my deepest convictions, viz. that reality always escapes prediction by taking a line which was simply not in your thought at all…. At any rate, this book excites me. (CLII, "To His Brother (W)," March 21, 1940; 369-370.)

To his credit, Lewis accepted the limits of his theology. Even if he actually had been given a tour of Heaven and Hell, he knew what the results would be. Letting Dante speak for him:

> Within that heav'n which most receives His light,
> Was I, and saw such things as man nor knows
> Nor skills to tell, returning from that height;
>
> For when our intellect is drawing close
> To its desire, its paths are so profound
> That memory cannot follow where it goes.
> (*Paradise*, Canto I, 4-9; 53)

The apostle Paul would agree:

> I know a man in Christ who fourteen years ago was caught up to the third heaven – whether in the body or out of the body I do not know, God knows. And I know that this man was caught up into Paradise – whether in the body or out of the body I do not know, God knows – and he heard things that cannot be told, which man may not utter. (2 Cor 12:2-4)

And so just as Lewis refused to speculate about the "geography" of the spirit world, he also refused to let predestination restrict the possibility of universal salvation, even while not yielding to the allure of universalism. What Lewis did claim to know is that every human has the awesome responsibility and precious gift of choice. In each human life, time and eternity touch, and the choices a person makes in time determine where a person spends eternity. Choice is, Lewis concluded, "the gift whereby ye most resemble your Maker and are yourselves parts of eternal reality" (122).

POST-DEATH SANCTIFICATION

Lewis also understood the descent of Christ as the opportunity for God to finish his purifying work in human souls who have chosen him. The process of sanctification is depicted through the Ghost-Spirit conversations, the instructions of McDonald, and even the landscape of Heaven. At the heart of this doctrine is the cleansing of the soul, and Lewis believed this process would allow the uniqueness of each person to develop. But just when and how does this process take place in a person's life, and does God accomplish it alone, or with human participation?

First, sanctification is not the same as justification. Lewis avoids sorting through the differing definitions for these concepts current in the Church, and in content to understand justification as the forgiveness of sins through faith in Christ's atonement. With that accomplished, the next part of redemption is the removal of all sinfulness from the soul. (The body will be resurrected.) To be forgiven is wonderful, but now inner, actual change needs to begin. The process begins with new life within from God, and will not be complete until the soul is cleansed and transformed.

HOW SANCTIFICATION DEPENDS UPON US

The title of this chapter ("Understanding Choice") names our part in sanctification; we choose to yield to God. "We, at most, allow it to be done to us" (MC: 150). And yet, can it be true that a feeble creature of clay can resist the Almighty himself; can in a sense "defeat" God? The irony, the staggering implications were not lost on Lewis.

> In creating beings with free will, omnipotence from the outset submits to the possibility of such defeat. What you call defeat, I call miracle: for to make things which are not Itself, and thus to become, in a sense, capable of being resisted by its own handiwork, *is the most astonishing and unimaginable of all the feats we attribute to the Deity* (PP: 127, emphasis mine).

But there is more to be said about what choice involves. Since Lewis is focusing upon souls near the end of their choices, it's easy to overlook life back on earth. When a person does choose to become a Christian and asks God to both forgive and remove sin, the result (for most, at least) is not instant perfection. Rather, God begins to reveal things unnoticed, or forgotten, or not yet surrendered to him. And once the "skeletons in the closet" are brought out into the light, the pattern of sanctification seems to require a person to admit to their presence, and begin to struggle with them. This is where the spiritual disciplines come in, and by them the partnership of human choice and divine grace grows in strength and understanding.

WHEN IS SANCTIFICATION COMPLETE?

Lewis did not (as far as I can discover) weigh the arguments for the complete sanctification of the soul before death as Wesleyan theology holds. He simply assumes we will leave this life still imperfect, but he balances this by exhorting the believer to make as much progress as possible before death. "The job will not be completed in this life: but He means to get us as far as possible before death" (MC: 159).

Most believers, and theologians, agree with Lewis that sinless perfection before death, if not impossible, is not experienced by most humans. But since most Protestants wish to avoid the doctrine of Purgatory which they associate with Catholicism, only one option is left for them: death itself must be the point when sanctification becomes complete. But Lewis rejects this position because he maintains that while God is the one who sanctifies us, he will only do so when we allow him. The dialogue between the Ghost with the red lizard and the angel is the strongest expression of this; the angel insists that he can do nothing without the Ghost's permission. "The metamorphosis of the lizard into the stallion was meant to symbolise perfect sublimation, after painful struggle and agonising surrender, not by ordinary psychological law but by supernatural Grace" (CLIII, "To Mr. Pitman," February 13, 1958; 920). So then, the death of the body when many are unconscious, senile or mentally confused is hardly the best time for divine grace and human permission to work together to perfect the soul.

Since Lewis felt complete cleansing from sin before death unlikely, nor will leaving the body somehow purify the soul, sanctification after death is the only option left. And this is how Lewis understood Purgatory; in essence, nothing more than the completion of sanctification after death. So then, whenever this process begins in each human life, no matter how many moral choices are involved, and whenever it ends, before or after the resurrection, before or during the judgment, God will change each person who yields to him until the sinful nature inherited from Adam is removed and the natural life is transformed.

IS PERFECTION POSSIBLE?

Is Lewis expecting too much? After all, to be a human is to stumble and fall again and again. This world is full of temptations and humans are full of limitations, not to mention the sinful nature that has come down to every person from the fall. I can understand why some of my students have expressed the opinion that believers will never be perfect. If they mean believers will never become the same as God, that's certainly true. But the Bible does promise in many places that by the grace of God, humans and sin will forever part company.

Many of those same students have the idea that getting rid of the body will take care of the problem. And I can understand why they feel that way, since college life often brings struggles with raging hormones or eating disorders. Lewis spoke to this issue in the first meeting with his tour guide. MacDonald did agree that some would be lost through "the undignified vices" or "mere sensuality," but the greater dangers by far were diseases of the soul, especially pride (69). Bodily appetites have their limits because the body is limited, but what are the limits of "spiritual sins" such as anger, jealousy, slander and pride?

Whatever the sin, or its source, Lewis will allow no compromise. Only a perfected human can hope to fellowship with a perfect God in the ages to come. Jesus says, in effect,

> If you let me, I will make you perfect. The moment you put yourself in My hands, that is what you are in for. Nothing less, or other, than that. You have free will, and if you choose, you can push Me away. But if you do not push Me away, understand that I am going to see this job through. Whatever suffering it may cost you in your earthly life, whatever inconceivable purification it may cost you after death, whatever it costs Me, I will never rest, nor let you rest, until you are literally perfect—until my Father can say without reservation that He is well pleased with you, as He said He was well pleased with me. This I can do and will do. But I will not do anything less (MC: 158).

But how does God accomplish the work of sanctification? Lewis wisely leaves the "how" of divine work in the realm of divine mystery. When the man with the red lizard finally gave his consent to be sanctified, the lizard of lust was "killed" and then transformed. How God accomplished that is beyond human understanding.

> You see, we are now trying to understand, and to separate into water-tight compartments, what exactly God does and what man does when God and man are working together. And, of course, we begin by thinking it is like two men working together, so that you could say, "He did this bit and I did that." But this way of thinking breaks down. God is not like that. He is inside you as well as outside: even if we could understand who did what, I do not think human language could properly express it (MC: 115-116).

It is enough, Lewis held, to believe that he can, and will, perfect us. Our part is to let him do his work, and to let him help us do ours.

CONCLUSION

What did Lewis accomplish by describing this imaginary journey? This was his opportunity to work through a number of theological issues and share his conclusions with his readers. The awesome responsibility of choice, Heaven and Hell, the nature of God, and sanctification as a process that continues after death are all explained. And by focusing upon people and places, Lewis made his theology come alive so that readers can feel in their hearts as well as understand with their minds what Lewis believed.

BUILDING ON *THE SCREWTAPE LETTERS*

When Lewis wrote *The Screwtape Letters* for *The Guardian*, the climax of that fictional correspondence came when the Patient died in battle, opened his eyes in Heaven and saw for the first time those in the spirit world who had a part in his life: Wormwood (a fallen angel), good angels, and finally God himself. But just safely arriving in Heaven wasn't enough for Lewis; there will be another chapter in the Patient's life after he has died.

> Pains he may still have to encounter, but they *embrace* those pains. They would not barter them for any earthly pleasure. All the delights of sense or heart or intellect with which you could once have tempted him, even the delights of virtue itself, now seem to him in comparison but as the half-nauseous attractions of a raddled harlot would seem to a man who hears that his true beloved whom he has loved all his life and whom he had believed to be dead is alive and even now at his door (SL 145).

With this paragraph, Lewis brought Screwtape's correspondence to a close, and at the same time, prepared his readers for a most unusual bus ride.

THE NATURE OF GOD

Lewis emphatically stressed through the landscape of Heaven that God is real. God not only exists, He is more real than anyone or anything else. He is, always has been, and always will be, reality itself. To choose God is to choose reality, and to embrace reality brings the truth about Him and one's own self. To turn away from God is to reject reality and construct instead a state of mind, a "house" which can't keep out the rain.

Lewis makes a valuable contribution to theology by stressing the reality of God even more than his holiness. Holiness is really wholeness, and he well understood that all evil is derivative; good that has become twisted and perverted. This theology lies behind Screwtape's complaint that devils find their work so difficult because God has created everything and devils can't create anything. They are reduced to taking what the Enemy has made and somehow convincing humans to misuse it.

God is merciful and loving, but also holy. He will resurrect our bodies so they will become spiritual bodies that can enter Heaven. And he will, if we allow Him, take what has become twisted and stunted, and kill it, so that it may be reborn in the full strength and beauty for which God designed it. But there can be no compromise, no marriage of reality and unreality. Heaven is offered on those terms alone.

Four Theological Issues

The Problem of Salvation

Perhaps I've gone out on a theological limb with the claim that this is Lewis' most important theological contribution, but so far, I see no reason to change my mind. And I'll go out a little further on that limb and claim that Christianity's biggest stumbling block is the doctrine that salvation only comes through Christ, even though millions have never had the opportunity to hear of his existence, much less to accept or reject him.

If the descent of Christ into Hades is a timeless event that gives everyone (finally) the opportunity to accept him, then such promises as "Seek and you will find" and "I will draw everyone to me" are kept. No one is lost but those who choose self over God, and no one can say "I never had a chance." God is reality, he is merciful, he is holy, and he is just. In explaining salvation, Lewis has also defended the character of God, thereby removing the stumbling block that has turned so many away from a Christianity that seemed to unfairly consign so many to Hell.

But if the theology of Lewis is sound, the language he used to express it, or more accurately, failed to use, will leave many evangelicals disappointed. We (yes, I include myself here) look for such expressions as "repent," "born again," and salvation by faith alone, to mention a few. The apostate bishop once believed (but was he born again?), but Lewis does not describe most of the characters we meet in this book as born-again believers.

Elsewhere in his theological writing, Lewis did clearly state that new life from Christ is our only hope. But to start describing how each of his characters repented, believed, were born again, and so forth, would have made the journey very tedious and repetitive indeed. We can safely assume that each character (and each person in the world) can only find new life and reach complete sanctification through Christ. The fateful decision to begin or refuse that process was the focus of this book, not what comes afterward.

The approach Lewis used also shows how what appears to be an oversimplification in the teaching of Jesus will become reality. At the present time, humanity exists on this planet in a bewildering complexity of cultures, religious beliefs, and no beliefs at all. Yet Jesus spoke (in his parables) of all humanity as somehow reduced in the future to simply good fish or bad fish, sheep or goats, wheat or weeds. And he gave the solution when he promised that "everyone will be drawn to me," implying an encounter leading to a decision. Lewis took that prediction seriously, and (once again at the risk of repeating myself) so he focused his descriptions on various souls making that most important choice.

THE PROBLEM OF SANCTIFICATION

Not many believers, even deeply committed Christians, would claim to be free from all sin in this life. Lewis certainly thought that would be highly improbable, if not impossible, given the fallen world in which we find ourselves. But no sin can remain in Heaven. The only possible solution for Lewis is the completion of sanctification after death. Just dying doesn't remove sin. Heaven must accomplish that, and only with our permission.

Once again, Lewis used simplification to his advantage. Each character seems to have only one sin holding him or her back; real life is much more complicated than that. What believer wouldn't be overjoyed to find only one sin left to be dealt with after death? But the principle is the important thing; a sin must be acknowledged and the soul yielded without reservation to God so He can do what only He can do. Lewis expected his readers to understand that the process would be repeated as often as necessary, and that the only acceptable conclusion to it would be the complete purification and transformation of the soul. Any committed believer, Lewis adds, would have it no other way.

THE PROBLEM OF JUDGMENT

The Bible offers so many different perspectives on this topic that most believers just give up and leave the details to God. Some texts speak of every idle word being judged, others emphasize how we treated each other, still others mention the motivations of our heart, and John writes that (in some sense) the judgment has already taken place (John 3:18). Can these and still other descriptions of the judgment be somehow integrated into a coherent theology?

For Lewis, the answer is yes. Everyone will stand before Christ and there is no escaping this confrontation. Or, in the words of Jesus, "When I am lifted up from the earth, I will draw all men to myself" (John 12:32) and "Everyone will be salted with fire" (Mark 9:49). The response of each person; the soul shaped by actions, words and motivations during one's life, will bring surrender to that cleansing fire, or flight from unbearable truth.

Lewis found the opportunity to describe this final judgment when he concluded *The Chronicles of Narnia*. As Narnia is being eaten by huge dragons and lizards, all of the animals run for their lives ahead of them. But there is no escape. The only safe place is through the door of a stable*, and Aslan himself is standing beside the door. And so the animals came...

> But as they came right up to Aslan one or other of two things happened
> to each of them. They all looked straight in his face; I don't think they
> had any choice about that. And when some looked, the expression of
> their faces changed terribly—it was fear and hatred...but others looked

in the face of Aslan and loved him, though some of them were very frightened at the same time (*The Last Battle, 153-154*).

And so this meeting, good news to some and confrontation to others, simultaneously solves these three theological issues for Lewis. Everyone who hasn't yet heard the good news now meets Jesus. In his presence, salvation is offered, sanctification as well, until the soul is made whole, and those who refuse the fire/light/truth are judged. They have chosen their final state and their destination.

THE PROBLEM OF THE BODY

Only at the end of the journey does Lewis turn to this aspect of a person; he's much more concerned about the soul. When the man with the lizard of lust is transformed, Lewis takes the opportunity to point out that problems of the body (though the soul is certainly involved as well) are also addressed in God's sanctification of the individual. Even the body itself, though now too weak to enter Heaven, will be transformed in the resurrection of the dead.

And so Lewis envisages all humanity being offered (or confronted) with the ultimate choice, The choice that is the culmination of all the choices a person has made. That choice is also the opportunity for salvation that God in his mercy extends to all. The right choice will result in the transformation of the soul into spirit, and the physical body will be raised as a spiritual body. No wonder Lewis was enthralled with the promises of Christianity, once he finally made the right choice.

THE MORNING AND THE NIGHT

Enough speculation about time, eternity and heavenly places. Before the dream is over, Lewis points the reader to the mountains where sunrise is about to dawn (and when night in all its finality will descend upon the grey town). Now, while time still allows for the freedom of choice, make the right choice. Lewis is urgent; "Heaven will not wait forever". As he gazed at the face of his guide,

> I saw there something that sent a quiver through my whole body... His face flushed with a new light... The eastern side of every tree-trunk grew bright... All the time there had been bird noises, trillings, chatterings, and the like; but now suddenly the full chorus was poured from every branch; cocks were crowing, there was music of hounds, and horns, above all this ten thousand tongues of men and woodland angels and the wood itself sang... "Sleepers awake!"... One dreadful glance over my shoulder I essayed—not long enough to see (or did I see?) the rim of the sunrise that shoots Time dead with golden arrows and puts to

flight all phantasmal shapes... "The morning! The morning!" I cried, "I am caught by the morning and I am a ghost" (124-125).

Dante tells us what the light of that morning will bring to those souls who are ready.

> And so my mind, bedazzled and amazed,
>   Stood fixed in wonder, motionless, intent,
>
> And still my wonder kindled as I gazed.
>   That light doth so transform a man' whole bent
>   That never to another sight or thought
>   Would he surrender, with his own consent;
> For everything the will has ever sought
>   Is gathered there, and there is every quest
>   Made perfect, which apart from it falls short.
>   (*Paradise*, Canto xxxiii. 97-105: 346)

In the last analysis, the theology of Lewis is a "mere theology;" beneath all the landscapes, characters, and dialogues lies a simple, uncomplicated message. The only hope of salvation, complete purification, and resurrection lies in God. He cannot change his holy character to suit each person's demands, but he will change those who allow him, and he will welcome those he has changed into fellowship with one another and with him. And then, at last, what humans were created for, including the individuality of each person, will find its fullest expression, to our highest joy and to His eternal glory.

Lewis has set before us a journey of hope. The "Sociology" part ends on a glorious note, with Sarah Smith portraying what a cleansed and glorified human will become. The "Geography" part climaxes with the revelation of just how small Hell really is, how enormous Heaven is, how Hell cannot affect Heaven, and the good news that One has descended into Hades and now has authority over it (and the grave). And the Theology of the book brings the most hopeful message of all: no one will be excluded from the message of salvation.

So ends "the great divorce." Heaven and Hell can never be married; the divorce is permanent. Yet, there will be "marriages" of another sort. God will accomplish the perfection of souls that yield to him, and "marry" them with resurrected bodies. Next, "Then the new earth and sky, the same yet not the same as these, will rise in us as we have risen in Christ" (LM 124). Finally, the highest and eternal marriage. In the NT, Jesus comes as a thief for those not expecting him, but as the bridegroom for his own. And then, the great feast at the marriage supper of the Lamb.

Every disease that submits to a cure shall be cured. (119)

APPENDICES:

Appendix I: Summary of Characters

The twenty Ghosts, and the Spirits who met some of them, are listed and numbered in order of appearance, by description or name when available, the sin(s) that they are struggling with, and the approximate space Lewis devoted to them. Some Ghosts appear twice so their first number is used again as a reminder that we have met them before. I have included the length of the meetings because I believe the space Lewis devoted to an encounter is a good indication of the importance Lewis gave to the subjects being discussed. The eight most important entries (four or more pages) are marked with an asterisk.

	__Persons__	__Sin__	__Space Given__
	Chapter One		
1 & 2	A man and woman leave the line	Wounded pride	1/3 page
3	Short man disapproving of Lewis	Superiority complex	2/3 page
4	Big Man	Self-righteous	1/2 page
5 &6	Unisex couple	Romance over Heaven	1/6 page
7	Cheated woman	Impatience, temper	1/3 page
8	Poet	Self-centered/Reputation	1 page
	Chapter Two		
8	Poet (continued)	Self-centered/Reputation	1 1/2 pages
9	Intelligent Man (Ikey*)	Materialism/ Economic reform of Hell	4 1/2 pages
10	Fat, clean-shaven man (Episcopal Ghost)	Apostate/heresy	2/3 page
	Chapter Three		
11	Respectable Ghost	Pride (Social Status)	1/3 page

C. S. Lewis Goes to Heaven

	Persons	Sin	Space Given
	Chapter Four 4		
	Big Man (cont'd)/ Spirit named Len*	Self-righteous	4 1/4 pages
	Chapter Five		
10	Episcopal Ghost /Spirit named Dick*	Apostate/Heresy, Theological reform of Hell	8 1/4 pages
	Chapter Six		
9	Ikey (continued)	Materialism/Economic reform of Hell	2 1/2 pages
	Chapter Seven		
12.	Hard-bitten Ghost	Cynicism	3 3/4 pages
	Chapter Eight		
13	Well-dressed Ghost/Spirit	Shame/Self-centered	3 1/4 pages
	Chapter Nine		
14	Grumbling Ghost/Spirit	Complaining	1 page
15	Flirtatious Ghost	Relations with others	2/3 page
16	Artist Ghost/Spirit*	Pride/Artistic reputation	4 pages
	Chapter Ten		
17	Robert's wife Ghost/ Hilda, Robert's mother Spirit*	Possessive "love"	5 pages
	Chapter Eleven		
18	Pam Ghost/Pam's brother Spirit*	Possessive "love"	5 1/2 pages
19	Ghost + lizard/Burning Angel*	Lust	6 2/3 pages
	Chapters Twelve & Thirteen		
20	Frank + Tragedian*/ Sarah Smith	Self-pity (Frank)	13 pages

Appendix II: Biblical References

Lewis enriches *The Great Divorce* through the use of many scriptures from both Old and New Testaments. But he doesn't cite chapter and verse for his references, he often quotes only part of a verse, and he frequently paraphrases a text. Since the references vary from direct quotations to allusions or even the use of Biblical imagery, identifying the scriptures Lewis had in mind can be difficult. These tables should help. (Page numbers are from *The Great Divorce*)

Table I: Biblical Quotations. These references are direct quotations; variations in wording are because Lewis and I used different translations.

Passage	Page	Speaker	Reference
1. White as snow	42	Spirit/Dick	Isa 1:18

Come now, let us argue it out, says the LORD: though your sins are like scarlet, they shall be like snow; though they are red like crimson, they shall become like wool.

2. Repent and believe	43	Spirit/Dick	Mark 1:15

The time is fulfilled, and the kingdom of God has come near; repent, and believe in the good news.

3. Prove all things	43	Episcopal Ghost	1 Thess 5:21

Test everything; hold fast to what is good. (Misused)

4. When I became a man I put away childish things	44	Episcopal Ghost	1 Cor 13:11

When I was a child, I spoke like a child, I thought like a child, I reasoned like a child; when I became a man, I put an end to childish ways. (RSV Misused)

5. Growing up to the measure of the stature of Christ	46	Episcopal Ghost	Eph 4:13

...until all of us come to the unity of the faith and of the knowledge of the Son of God, to maturity, to the measure of the full stature of Christ. (Misused)

6. Come and see	79	Spirit	John 1:39

He said to them, "Come and see." They came and saw where he was staying, and they remained with him that day. (NRSV)

Passage	Page	Speaker	Reference
7. It is sown a natural body, it is raised a spiritual body.	102	MacDonald	1 Cor 15:44

It is sown a physical body, it is raised a spiritual body. If there is a physical body, there is also a spiritual body.

| 8. I never knew you | 116 | Sarah Smith | Matt 7:23 |

Then I will declare to them, 'I never knew you; go away from me, you evildoers.'

Table II: Biblical References

This group contains references to identifiable Biblical texts that have been paraphrased or referred to rather than directly quoted.

Passage	Page(s)	Speaker	Reference
1. On one journey even your right hand and your right eye may be among the things you have to leave behind.	9, 10	Lewis	Matt 5:29-30; cf. 18:8-9

If your right eye causes you to sin, tear it out and throw it away; it is better for you to lose one of your members than for your whole body to be thrown into hell. And if your right hand causes you to sin, cut it off and throw it away; it is better for you to lose one of your members than for your whole body to go into Hell (Matt 5:29-30).

If your hand or your foot causes you to stumble, cut it off and throw it away; it is better for you to enter life maimed or lame than to have two hands or two feet and to be thrown into the eternal fire. And if your eye causes you to stumble, tear it out and throw it away; it is better for you to enter life with one eye than to have two eyes and to be thrown into the hell of fire (Matt 18:8-9).

2. I defied the whole chapter	41	Episcopal Ghost	1 Cor 15

The Episcopal Ghost is referring to his rejection of the resurrection; "the whole chapter" probably refers to the fifteenth chapter of 1 Corinthians, Paul's famous "resurrection chapter."

3. The valley of the Shadow of Death (also reversed as the Valley of the Shadow of Life)	67	MacDonald	Psa 23:4
	67, 77	MacDonald	

Even though I walk through the darkest valley, I fear no evil; for you are with me; your rod and your staff—they comfort me.

4. For all that can be shaken will be shaken and only the unshakeable remains.	68	MacDonald	Heb 12:27

This phrase, "Yet once more," indicates the removal of what is shaken—that is, created things—so that what cannot be shaken may remain.

	Passage	Page(s)	Speaker	Reference

5. Those who seek find. To 72 ~~ MacDonald Matt 7:8
those who knock it is
opened.

For everyone who asks receives, and everyone who searches finds, and for everyone
who knocks, the door will be opened.

6. Every natural love will 96 *105* MacDonald John 12:24
rise again and live for-
ever in this country: but
none will rise again
until it has been buried.

Very truly, I tell you, unless a grain of wheat falls into the earth and dies, it remains
just a single grain; but if it dies, it bears much fruit.

7. There is but one good: 96 *106* MacDonald Matt 19:17
that is God.

And he said to him, "Why do you ask me about what is good? There is only one who
is good. If you wish to enter into life, keep the commandments."

8. Poem for Ghost with 101-102 *113* Arch-Nature Psa 110:1-4
lizard (lust) of the Land

For the text of Psa 110:1-4, see pages 101-102.

9. Flesh and blood cannot 102 *114* MacDonald 1 Cor 15:50
come to the mountains

What I am saying, brothers and sisters, is this: flesh and blood cannot inherit the
kingdom of God, nor does the perishable inherit the imperishable.

10. Poem for Sarah Smith 117 *134* Bright Spirits Psa 91

For the text of Psa 91, see page 117.

11. There is no Spirit in 121 *139-40* MacDonald 1 Pet 3:18-20
prison to whom he did
not preach

For Christ also suffered for sins once for all, the righteous for the unrighteous, in
order to bring you to God. He was put to death in the flesh, but made alive in the

spirit, in which also he went and made a proclamation to the spirits in prison, who in former times did not obey, when God waited patiently in the days of Noah, during the building of the ark, in which a few, that is, eight persons, were saved through water.

| 12. | The Lord said we were from gods | 122 | MacDonald | John 10:34, Psa 82:6 |

Jesus answered, "Is it not written in your law, 'I said, you are gods'? (John 10:34)

I say, "You are gods, children of the Most High, all of you... (Psa 82:6)

Table III: Biblical Allusions

Here Lewis seems to reflect a Biblical text but the words are not close enough to identify with confidence a specific chapter and verse.

	Passage	Page	Speaker	Reference
1.	You shall see the face of God (Beatific Vision)	43	Spirit/Dick	cf. Rev 22:3-4; 1 Cor 13:12

Nothing accursed will be found there any more. But the throne of God and of the Lamb will be in it, and his servants will worship him; they will see his face, and his name will be on their foreheads (Rev 22:3-4).

12 For now we see in a mirror, dimly, but then we will see face to face (1 Cor 13:12).

	Passage	Page	Speaker	Reference
2.	Taste it like honey	44	Spirit/Dick	cf. Psa 34:8; Psa 119:103

O taste and see that the LORD is good; happy are those who take refuge in him (Psa 34:8).

How sweet are your words to my taste, sweeter than honey to my mouth! (Psa 119:103)

	Passage	Page	Speaker	Reference
3.	Be embraced by it as by a bridegroom	44	Spirit/Dick	cf. Isa 62:5

For as a young man marries a young woman, so shall your builder marry you, and as the bridegroom rejoices over the bride, so shall your God rejoice over you (Isa 62:5).

	Passage	Page	Speaker	Reference
4.	Your thirst shall be quenched	44	Spirit/Dick	cf. John 7:37-38; Rev 22:17

On the last day of the festival, the great day, while Jesus was standing there, he cried out, "Let anyone who is thirsty come to me and let the one who believes in me drink.

He who believes in me, as the scripture has said, 'Out of his heart shall flow rivers of living water'" (John 7:38).

The Spirit and the bride say, "Come." And let everyone who hears say, "Come." And let everyone who is thirsty come. Let anyone who wishes take the water of life as a gift (Rev 22:17).

Appendices

Passage	Page(s)	Speaker	Reference
5. The smoke of Hell goes up forever	58 57	Lewis	cf. Rev 14:11; 19:3

And the smoke of their torment goes up forever and ever. There is no rest day or night for those who worship the beast and its image and for anyone who receives the mark of its name" (Rev 14:11)

Once more they said, "Hallelujah! The smoke goes up from her forever and ever" (Rev 19:3)

6. Come and feed	79 84	Spirit	cf. John 21:12

Jesus said to them, "Come and have breakfast." Now none of the disciples dared to ask him, "Who are you?" because they knew it was the Lord (John 21:12).

7. I believe in a God of Love.	94 103	Pam	cf. 1 John 4:16

So we know and believe the love God has for us. God is love, and he who abides in love abides in God, and God abides in him (1 John 4:16 RSV). (Misused)

8. Sleepers awake!	125 145	All nature	cf. Eph 5:14

Everything exposed by the light becomes visible, for everything that becomes visible is light. Therefore it says, "Sleeper, awake! Rise from the dead, and Christ will shine on you" (Eph 5:14).

Table IV: Biblical Imagery.

Lewis uses Biblical metaphors and imagery in his dialogues and also his description of places.

Passage	Page	Speaker	Reference
1. Vast Abyss between the grey town and Paradise	22, 26, 120	Lewis	Luke 16:26

Besides all this, between you and us a great chasm has been fixed, so that those who might want to pass from here to you cannot do so, and no one can cross from there to us (Luke 16:26).

2. It will be dark presently	24	Intelligent Man	cf. John 9:4

We must work the works of him who sent me while it is day; night is coming when no one can work (John 9:4).

3. But we look on this spiritual city	24	Intelligent Man	Heb 11:6, cf. Heb 11:9-10 Heb 13:14 Rev 21:2-3

But as it is, they desire a better country, that is, a Heavenly one. Therefore God is not ashamed to be called their God; indeed, he has prepared a city for them (Heb 11:6).

By faith he stayed for a time in the land he had been promised, as in a foreign land, living in tents, as did Isaac and Jacob, who were heirs with him of the same promise. 10 For he looked forward to the city that has foundations, whose architect and builder is God (Heb 11:9-10).

For here we have no lasting city, but we are looking for the city that is to come (Heb 13:14).

And I saw the holy city, the new Jerusalem, coming down out of Heaven from God, prepared as a bride adorned for her husband. And I heard a loud voice from the throne saying, "See, the home of God is among mortals (Rev 21:2-3).

4. River and tree of golden apples	27, 38, 48-49	Lewis	cf. Rev 22:1-2

Then the angel showed me the river of the water of life, bright as crystal, flowing from the throne of God and of the Lamb through the middle of the street of the city. On either side of the river is the tree of life with its twelve kinds of fruit, producing its fruit each month; and the leaves of the tree are for the healing of the nations (Rev 22:1-2).

	Passage	Page	Speaker	Reference
5.	Ask for the Bleeding Charity	35 28	Spirit	cf. Rev 7:14

I said to him, "Sir, you are the one that knows." Then he said to me, "These are they who have come out of the great ordeal; they have washed their robes and made them white in the blood of the Lamb (Rev 7:14).

6.	White unicorns for future battle	62	Lewis	cf. Rev 19:11, 14

Then I saw Heaven opened, and there was a white horse! Its rider is called Faithful and True, and in righteousness he judges and makes war… And the armies of Heaven, wearing fine linen, white and pure, were following him on white horses (Rev 19:11, 14).

7.	The vale of misery turns out… to have been a well, —-the pools were full of water.	68 70	MacDonald	cf. Psa 84:6

As they go through the valley of Baca they make it a place of springs; the early rain also covers it with pools (Psa 84:6).

8.	He could have begun all over again like a little child…	71 73	MacDonald	cf. Mark 10:15

Truly I tell you, whoever does not receive the kingdom of God as a little child will never enter it (Mark 10:15).

9.	…And entered into joy	71 73	MacDonald	cf. Matt 25:21

His master said to him, 'Well done, good and trustworthy slave; you have been trustworthy in a few things, I will put you in charge of many things; enter into the joy of your master' (Matt 25:21).

10.	It will be cured when you come to the fountain	80 85	Spirit	cf. Rev 7:17

The Lamb at the center of the throne will be their shepherd, and he will guide them to springs of the water of life, and God will wipe away every tear from their eyes" (Rev 7:17)

Passage	Page	Speaker	Reference
11. And St. Paul too	121	Lewis	cf. 1 Tim 4:10

For to this end we toil and struggle, because we have our hope set on the living God, who is the Savior of all people, especially of those who believe (1 Tim 4:10). (Description of Paul as a universalist.)

Appendix III: Historical People and Literary References

Notable people, subjects and literary references in *The Great Divorce* are listed here in alphabetical order. The interested reader will find a wealth of information that was not given in the main discussion. I debated at times where something should go, but decided at last to put most non-essential material here so that the narrative would flow more smoothly. Following each entry is the chapter in GD and the page in this book where it first appears.

Achilles (Ch 9, p 38)

The great warrior of myth is immortalized in the *Iliad*, Homer's account of a part of the tenth and final year of the war between the countries of Greece and Troy. The war began when Paris abducted Helen of Troy from King Menelaus. The epic poem opens with the lines:

> Sing, goddess, the rage of Achilles the son of Peleus,
> the destructive rage that countless pains on the Achaeans...

"Wrath" is the first word of the Greek text, and the wrath of Achilles is thus announced as the main theme of the epic poem.

Achilles is angry because Agamemnon, the commander of the Greek forces at Troy, dishonored him by taking Briseis for himself, a slave woman that had been given to Achilles as a prize of war. Achilles became enraged and withdrew from the battle. Because of his wounded pride over a woman, his own people are nearly defeated by the Trojans. Achilles reenters the fighting when his close friend Patroclus is killed by the Trojan Hector. Achilles slaughters many Trojans and kills Hector. Priam, the father of Hector, ransoms his son's body and the *Iliad* concludes with the funeral of Hector. In Lewis' view, the pride of Achilles and the violence it begets earns him residence in the grey town.

Alice (Ch 13, p 87)

Lewis is referring to Alice, the character of *Alice's Adventures in Wonderland*, who followed the White Rabbit into a burrow and underwent a number of changes in her size during her adventures in Wonderland. First a bottle with "Drink me" on the label made her smaller, then she ate a cake that made her more than nine feet tall. Next, the White Rabbit's fan brought her back down to a very small size again, and before too long, a little bottle in the Rabbit's house brought her to gigantic size once again. Next, pebbles that turned into little cakes reduced her size to three inches, and in that state she came across a caterpillar sitting upon a mushroom about her height. Their conversation was rather unsettling, given the cranky mood of the caterpillar, but as it crawled away, it informed Alice that one side of the mushroom would make her smaller, and the other side would make her larger. And so Alice finally managed to control her size by taking along with her a piece from each side of the mushroom as she continued her adventures.

Carroll wrote an acrostic poem in which the first letter of each line spelled out the name of the young girl whose name he would use in his stories:

A boat, beneath a sunny sky,
Lingering onward dreamily
In an evening of July –

Children three that nestle near,
Eager eye and willing ear,
Pleased a simple tale to hear –

Long has paled that summer sky:
Echoes fade and memories die:
Autumn frosts have slain July.

Still she haunts me, phantomwise,
Alice moving under skies
Never seen by waking eyes.

Children yet, the tale to hear,
Eager eye and willing ear,
Lovingly shall nestle near.

In a Wonderland they lie,
Dreaming as the days go by.
Dreaming as the summers die.

Ever drifting down the stream –
Lingering in the golden gleam –
Life, what is it but a dream?

Lewis Carroll was the pen name used by Reverend Charles Lutwidge Dodgson (1832-1898), the author of *Alice's Adventures in Wonderland* and lecturer in mathematics at Oxford University. The story began one summer day in 1862 when Dodgson and Reverend Robinson Duckworth rowed up the Thames river with three young girls who asked for a story: Lorina Charlotte Liddell (age 13), Alice Pleasance Liddell (10), and Edith Marie Liddell (8). The story enchanted the girls, and Alice asked Dodgson to write it down for her. He did so, and gave her the manuscript entitled *Alice's Adventures Under Ground* in 1864.

According to his diaries, Dodgson also showed the story to his friend George MacDonald; none other than Lewis' tour guide. His children also loved the story, and with MacDonald's urging, Dodgson published it in 1865 as *Alice's Adventures in Wonderland,* with illustrations by John Tenniel. The adventures of Alice have enjoyed tremendous popularity, as seen by the fact that the book never goes out of print and has now been translated into some 125 languages.

Anodos (Ch 9)

The wandering character in *Phantastes*, the book by MacDonald that meant so much to Lewis. His name means "path," from the combination of the Greek preposition "ana" (up) and the noun "hodos" (path, way, road, etc.) The "h" in "hodos" is signified by a breathing mark in Greek, so the word for road actually begins with the vowel "o" (omicron) under the breathing mark. When a preposition ending with a vowel is prefixed to a word beginning with a vowel, the vowel of the preposition is dropped to facilitate pronunciation. Hence, ana + odos becomes anodos.

Or, MacDonald may have intended just the opposite meaning for the name, since Anodos can also be the combination of the letter alpha prefixed to hodos. When the alpha is used to reverse the meaning of a word, it is called an "alpha privative." Thus "road" (odos) becomes "no road" (anodos), just as theist becomes atheist, etc. The "n" (Greek letter "nu") is added to separate the two vowels and so facilitate pronunciation, as in "a mistake" but "an error."

Anodos began his journey into fairy land by following a path but soon left it to travel in an easterly direction. His journeys took him in random directions so perhaps "pathless" would be the best interpretation of his name. Eventually his travels brought him to a little cottage with no windows. Entering, he found a woman cooking something in a little pot who fed him and gave him rest. Noticing the cottage had four doors, one in each wall, he tried each of them in turn, and found many strange adventures. He returned to the cottage each time, but when he resolved to go through the fourth door, the woman warned him against doing so.

Anodos rejected her warning, and stepped through the fourth door. The next thing he knew, he found himself lying on the floor of the cottage. No memory remained (if there ever had been any) of his experiences on the other side of the fourth door, and MacDonald gave no description. But the woman told Anodos she herself had to go through that door named Timeless to fetch him, else he would have never returned. And because she had gone through that door, the waters around the cottage on the isthmus would rise above the cottage and threaten to enter it. But if she kept the fire burning, they would not be able to come into it. After a year, the waters would subside and things would return to normal. What befell Anodos when he went through the fourth door is the only part of his journey that MacDonald does not describe, and Lewis understood him to mean that we cannot understand eternity while we are living in this world.

Archibald, Sir (Ch 9, 9)

The name Lewis gave to Sir Arthur Conan Doyle (May 22, 1859 –July 7, 1930). The pseudonym may indicate respect for a contemporary.

Lewis shared Doyle's fascination with the spirit world, but eventually managed to bring it under control, whereas Doyle did not. Nevertheless, Doyle did accomplish much, in addition to his detective stories. At the age of 40, he tried to enlist in the Boer War, but was rejected for being out of physical condition. But he did find a way to contribute as a doctor in Africa, and he was knighted (hence the "Sir') by King Edward VII in 1902 for service during the Boer War. He also volunteered to enlist in WWI, and made many recommendations which he thought would assist Britain in the struggle. Winston Churchill himself wrote Doyle to thank him for his ideas. After 1918, Doyle's focus on spiritualism largely eclipsed his writing career.

Lewis had a literary "grudge" against Doyle, though I don't think this explains Lewis "sending" him to the grey town. Writing to his brother Warren, Lewis commented, "In fact I don't like Doyle. Where his short stories deal with themes I like they usually leave me reflecting how much better almost any other writer wd. have done it" (CLII, "To His Brother," May 4, 1940; 410). Lewis could be a demanding literary critic, but Doyle's obsession with the afterlife, not his writing style, surely accounts for Lewis giving him permanent citizenship in the grey town.

On an interesting biographical note, one of Lewis' students was Roger Lancelyn Green (1918-1987). Lewis didn't wear a watch, and had a habit of borrowed Green's during class. They became life-long friends, and Green was often a guest at meetings of the Inklings. Green enjoyed the *Chronicles of Narnia*, and was a supporter and helpful critic of them. Lewis visited Green several times at Poulton Hall, his ancestral home. At his suggestion, Jack and Joy booked a cruise ship and visited the isles of Greece.

Green became, according to Hooper, the world's leading authority on Victorian children's books, and, ironically, was also an early member of the Sherlock Holmes Society of London. His son Richard eventually became the leading authority on Doyle and his fictional detective and set up a replica of Holmes's study at Poulton Hall (CLII: 1039-1043).

In *The Magician's Nephew*, Lewis relates Narnian chronology to earth's history by means of Doyle's famous detective. "In those days Mr. Sherlock Holmes was still living in Baker Street and the Bastables were looking for treasure in the Lewisham Road." (MN: 1) As Paul Ford explains, Lewis mentions Doyle "... to set the times. Since Narnia is a work of fiction, it really exists in the world of fiction in which Holmes is also real" (*Companion to Narnia*: 230).

Beatific Vision or Face of God (Ch 5, 29)

If the description of Heaven is difficult, and Lewis has warned us against those who would portray it by scenes of earthly beauty, how much more perilous must be the task of describing God himself. Surely this is one reason why symbols have been created. And yet, that face, above all worlds and all human thought, is the ultimate destiny, for joy or terror, for every human being. Life should therefore be lived with that destiny in mind.

In *Perelandra*, Ransom is privileged to have this experience and so (at least in fiction) joins the ranks (doubtless few in number) of mystics and saints who have briefly seen the indescribable. But Ransom first encounters the opposite vision, which Lewis calls the "Miserific vision," perhaps coining a new expression as he does so. Ransom comes upon his enemy in the story, now possessed by Satan, and the smiling expression on the face of Weston causes him to faint.

> As he lay there, still unable and perhaps unwilling to rise, it came into his mind that in certain old philosophers and poets he had read that the mere sight of the devils was one of the greatest among the torments of Hell. It had seemed to him till now merely a quaint fancy. And yet (as he now saw) even the children knew better: no child would have any difficulty in understanding that there might be a face the mere beholding of which was final calamity. The children, the poets, and the philosophers were right. As there is one Face above all worlds merely to see which is irrevocable joy, so at the bottom of all worlds that face is waiting whose sight alone is the misery from which none who beholds it can recover. And though there seemed to be, and indeed were, a thousand roads by which a man could walk through the world, there was not a single one which did not lead sooner or later either to the Beatific or Miserific Vision. He himself had, of course, seen only a mask or faint adumbration of it; even so, he was not quite sure that he would live (PER: 96).

Ransom did live, and successfully fought with Weston to help prevent *Perelandra* from falling. At the end of his experiences there, after ascending to a mountain top, he hears angelic voices speaking of a "Great Dance" and voicing praise to the Creator. The voices explain how God is at the center of all things, and how all things have their existence in him. "And now, by a transition which he did not notice, it seemed that what had begun as speech was turned into sight, or into something that can be remembered only as if it were seeing. He thought he saw the Great Dance" (PER: 187). Cords of moving light representing people, empires, worlds, truths, qualities—indeed, all of creation—moved together in divine harmony. And still the vision expanded; dimension after dimension was added, far beyond Ransom's ability to comprehend. And then,

> At the very zenith of complexity, complexity was eaten up and faded, as a thin white cloud fades into the hard blue burning of the sky, and a simplicity beyond all comprehension, ancient and young as spring, illimitable, pellucid, drew him with cords of infinite desire into its own stillness. He went up into such a quietness, a privacy, and a freshness that at the very moment when he stood farthest from our ordinary mode of being he had the sense of stripping off encumbrances and awaking from trance, and coming to himself (PER: 188).

Lewis gives no shape, size or color to the "simplicity beyond all comprehension," but he has already achieved more in the description of the Great Dance than most authors today would dare or could manage.

But the experience will be far from beatific for some. Just as Ransom could barely endure even the faintest impression of Satan's face in Weston, the face of God will bring terror to all who refuse to yield to him. When Lewis concluded the *Chronicles of Narnia*, the history of that world ended with a final judgment, as will ours. And once again, the focus of Lewis is upon that face which all must encounter.

> But as they came right up to Aslan one or other of two things happened to each of them. They all looked straight *in his face*; *I don't think they had any choice about that*. And when some looked, the expression of their faces changed terribly—it was fear and hatred; except that, on the faces of Talking Beasts, the fear and hatred lasted only for a fraction of a second. You could see that they suddenly ceased to be *Talking* Beasts. They were just ordinary animals. And all the creatures who looked at Aslan that way swerved to their right, his left, and disappeared into his huge black shadow, which (as you have heard) streamed away to the left of the doorway. The children never saw them again. I don't know what became of them. But the others looked *in the face of Aslan* and loved him, though some of them were very frightened at the same time (LB: 153-154, emphases mine).

Lewis had a way of getting down to the essentials. Many have a mental image of billions of people waiting for ages to appear before the Judge, who will then review each day of their lives. Not Lewis; the judgment will be simple and quick; how people have shaped themselves by all of their decisions determines whether that face is a sight of joy or unbearable terror. Either way, the result will be permanent.

> In the end that Face which is the delight or the terror of the universe must be turned upon each of us either with one expression or with the other, either conferring glory inexpressible or inflicting shame that can never be cured or disguised... It is written that we shall "stand before" Him, shall appear, shall be inspected. The promise of glory is the promise, almost incredible and only possible by the work of Christ, that some of us, that any of us who really chooses, shall actually survive that examination, shall find approval, shall please God ("Weight of Glory" in WG: 39).

Just as Lewis imagined through Ransom what the experience might be like, so Dante applied his genius to the same task. In the words of Barbara Reynolds, who finished the translation and notes of *Paradise* so ably begun by Dorothy L. Sayers:

> Heaven has, of course, always been inconceivable... Of the few poets or prophets who have undertaken to describe it, even fewer have dared to keep us there for long... Dante alone has had the astonishing courage to take us into Heaven and keep us there for thirty-three long cantos, building it to his ecstatic climax without introducing any grandiose events, and scenery, or any incantatory dreaminess which suspends disbelief by lulling the wits to sleep (*Paradise*, Introduction: 19-20).

And just what did he see after reaching the tenth and highest heaven? With Ransom on Perelandra, he saw in the light of God the form of all creation. Then, God himself, one and yet three in Persons. These he saw, but only because by successive transformations he became finally able to see.

> Not that the living light I looked on wore
> > More semblances than one, which cannot be,
> > For it is always what it was before;
>
> But as my sight by seeing learned to see,
> > The transformation which in me took place
> > Transformed the single changeless form for me.
>
> That light supreme, within its fathomless
> > Clear substance, showed to me three spheres, which bare
> > Three hues distinct, and occupied one space;

> The first mirrored the next, as though it were
>> Rainbow from rainbow, and the third seemed flame
>> Breathed equally from each of the first pair.
>>> (*Paradise*, Canto xxxiii. 109-120: 346)

Next, Dante also saw the image of man, for God himself became incarnate as man.

> The sphering thus begot, perceptible
>> In Thee like mirrored light, now to my view -
>> When I had looked on it a little while -
>
> Seemed in itself, and in its own self-hue,
>> Limned with our image; for which cause mine eyes
>> Were altogether drawn and held thereto.
>>> (*Paradise*, Canto xxxiii. 127-132: 346)

And then the experience, beyond Dante's capacity to describe further, is over. What Lewis described as "simplicity beyond all comprehension" Dante rendered as three spheres of three colors, and the image of man, yet in one space. Simplicity indeed. And so, while we are in this world and in these bodies, this must suffice, for now we see "in a mirror, dimly." But we have the promise of Paul to sustain us: "but then face to face" (1 Cor 13:12), and from John, "They shall see his face" (Rev 22:4).

Beatrice (Ch 9, 6)

Beatrice Portinari (1266–1290), was born in Florence, Italy, and Dante first met her when his father took him to the Portinari house for a May Day party in 1274. He was nine and she was eight, but despite their age he was smitten by her, and secretly loved her from that time on, writing some twenty years later *La Vita Nuovo (The New Life)* to express what she meant to him. Somehow, even at that young age, "Beatrice and his love for her were the medium of his moral reform and of his religious salvation" (Sayers, *Paradise*: 49). In his own words,

> I say that whenever and wherever she appeared, in the hope of that most priceless salute, I had no longer an enemy in the world, such a flame of charity was kindled within me, making me forgive every one who had offended me; and had I then been asked for any favor upon earth, I should, with looks clothed with humility, have answered nought but "Love." (*La Vita Nuovo:* 13-14.)

In *The Divine Comedy*, Dante's first guide is Virgil, but because he was a pagan, although a virtuous pagan, he is unable to lead Dante into Heaven. When Dante and Virgil ascend to the top of Mount Purgatory and enter Paradise, they encounter a beautiful procession. Beatrice, his new tour guide, is approaching. In the notes to her translation of Dante, Sayers refers to this procession as "The Pageant of the Sacrament" because it celebrates the indwelling of Christ in His creation through his divine and human natures, and because the Eucharist is both a symbol of that union and the place where Christians participate in it (Sayers, *Purgatory*, 303).

> The beauteous pageantry flamed forth on high
> Far brighter than the brightest moon could shine
> At her mid-month in a clear midnight sky.
>
> I turned, all wonder, looking for a sign
> From my good Virgil, but his answering glance
> Showed a bewilderment not less than mine.
>
> (Sayers, *Purgatory*, Canto 29: 52-57; 299)

Virgil is unable to help Dante, because they are now seeing Christian mysteries which are beyond the pagan's understanding. Another guide must now lead Dante.

In the next Canto, Beatrice appears to Dante "cloaked in green." Turning once again to his guide, he finds that Virgil has disappeared, a fact which reduces him to tears. But Beatrice tells him not to weep, and thereafter becomes his guide and much more; explaining, rebuking, encouraging, but always helping him until he is able to perceive the mysteries of Heaven on his own. "She is the image by which Dante perceives such things and her function in the poem is to bring him to that state in which he is able to perceive them directly" (Sayers, *Paradise*, 49). Lewis follows Dante's example, acknowledging MacDonald's life-long spiritual influence upon him by choosing him to be his guide and the interpreter of what he sees and hears.

Blake, William (Preface, 3)

"Blake" is the very first word of GD, and Lewis is referring to William Blake (November 28, 1757- August 12, 1827), the Romantic poet and mystic. Blake was born in London to a middle-class family, apprenticed to an engraver, and admitted to the Royal Academy of Art in 1779.

A true mystic, even as a child Blake reported seeing "a tree filled with angels" and when his younger brother Robert died at the age of 19, he claimed to see his spirit rise to heaven "clapping its hands for joy." Soon thereafter, Robert revealed to him a method of Illuminated Printing in a dream, using etched copper plates for printing pages which were then colored by hand.

Blake used this technique to publish *The Marriage* and provided engravings for many other books, including Milton's *Paradise Lost*.

In 1789, Blake joined with followers of Swedenborg and signed a list of thirty-two resolutions supporting the founding of a New Church, since they believed the Anglican Church had been spoiled by a repressive clergy and incomprehensible doctrines. Yet, he soon attacked Swedenborg's theology, the cosmology of Milton, as well as the morality of the established church for being too rigid and repressive.

Blake published *The Marriage of Heaven and Hell* sometime between 1790-1793 as a work of prose and two poems published by means of twenty-seven engraved, colored plates. In his opening argument, Blake asserts on plate three:

> Without Contraries is no progression. Attraction and Repulsion, Reason and Energy, Love and Hate, are necessary to Human existence. From these contraries spring what the religious call Good & Evil. Good is the passive that obeys Reason. Evil is the active springing from Energy. Good is Heaven. Evil is Hell.

On plate four, he further explained these "contraries:"

> All Bibles or sacred codes have been the causes of the following Errors:
> 1. That Man has two real existing principles: Viz: a Body & a Soul.
> 2. That Energy, call'd Evil, is alone from the Body, & that Reason, call'd Good, is alone from the Soul.
> 3. That God will torment Man in Eternity for following his Energies.
>
> But the following Contraries to these are True:
>
> 1. Man has no Body distinct from his Soul; for that call'd Body is a portion of Soul discern'd by the five Senses, the chief inlets of Soul in this age.
> 2. Energy is the only life, and is from the Body; and Reason is the bound or outward circumference of Energy.
> 3. Energy is Eternal Delight.

The Marriage still generates controversy among scholars; its structure, sources, purpose, and message are all debated. Lewis himself wasn't sure he understood him. More than one critic has concluded that Blake was insane, and yet he could write:

> To see a world in a grain of sand
> And heaven in a wild flower
> Hold infinity in the palm of your hand

And eternity in an hour.
(The first four lines of "Auguries of Innocence")

Bus Driver, The (Ch 1, p 11)

Confirmation that Lewis modeled the Bus Driver after Dante's angel comes in his correspondence. In his words: "...the bus-driver in the Divorce is certainly, and consciously, modeled on the angel at the gates of Dis, just as the meeting of the Tragedian with his wife is consciously modeled on that of Dante & Beatrice at the end of the *Purgatorio*" (CLIII, "To William Kinter," March 3, 1953; 313-4). A year later, Lewis wrote to Mr. Kinter again, saying "The closest conscious debt to Dante in *G. Divorce* is the angel who drives the bus: of *Inferno* IX, 79-102" (CLIII, "To William L. Kinter," July 30, 1954; 498).

Cézanne (Ch 9, p 46)

Paul Cézanne (French), Jan. 19, 1839 - Oct. 22, 1906, was one of the greatest of the Postimpressionists. His work influenced many modern styles, especially Cubism, and he is regarded as the father of modern painting. In 1872, Camille Pissarro advised him to "care more for outward reality than for his inner passions." He took this advice to heart and learned to "suggest the effect of light and shade through the spots of impressionistic technique" (Venturi: 62). In the opinion of another critic, Cezanne was "true to the Impressionist doctrine in paying great attention to light" (Roberts: 11). It's hardly surprising that Sargent was attracted to, and imitated, his work.

"City of God" (Ch 5, p 29)

These words come from the first line of Samuel Johnson's hymn of the same name.

> City of God, how broad and far,
> Outspread thy walls sublime!
> The true thy chartered freemen are,
> Of every age and clime.
>
> One holy Church, one army strong;
> One steadfast, high intent;
> One working band, one harvest song,
> One King omnipotent.
>
> How purely hath thy speech come down
> From man's primeval youth!

How grandly hath thine empire grown
Of freedom, love and truth!

How gleam thy watch fires through the night
With never fainting ray!
How rise thy towers, serene and bright,
To meet the dawning day!

In vain the surge's angry shock,
In vain the drifting sands;
Unharmed upon the eternal Rock
The eternal City stands.

(*Hymns of the Spirit*, 1864; www.cyberhymnal.org.)
Music by Thomas Haweis, words by Samuel Johnson.

The words reflect Saint Augustine's *The City of God*. The apostasy of the Episcopal Ghost has made him so spiritually blind that he has come to regard the grey town as the church.

Claude (chxx, 46)

See Monet, Claude

Coriolanus (Ch 9, p 38)

The "grandeur" of Coriolanus refers to the haughty spirit of a fictional character described by the Greek historian Plutarch. Caius Martius is a distinguished Roman soldier whose bravery accounts for the defeat of the Volscians, enemies of Rome. To honor his heroic conquest of the city Corioli, he is given the honorific title of Coriolanus. Plutarch describes him as supporting the Roman aristocracy. But when accused of misappropriating public funds, he turned against Rome and threatened to attack Rome with the help of the Volscians. The militaristic pride of Coriolanus earned him, in the view of Lewis, residence in the grey town, along with Achilles and Tamberlaine.

Apart from Plutarch, Lewis' literary background also served to bring this character from the classics to his attention; this time through Shakespeare's play *Coriolanus*. This was his last tragedy, written around 1605, and Shakespeare emphasized the pride of Coriolanus and his contempt for the Roman masses. Lewis recalls discussing this play in 1924 when he spent a weekend in London with two friends: Leo Baker, who had a brief career on the stage, and Cecil Harwood. After watching a (bad) performance of *As You Like It* at the New Oxford Theater, they mulled over just how much Shakespeare believed in such characters as Romeo and Coriolanus, and how often he was actually writing tongue-in-cheek (AMR: 337). Two years later, he attended a performance of Coriolanus ("bad beyond description!") and even skimmed the play before attending (AMR: 409).

While Shakespeare closely followed Plutarch's story, he also filled out many characters and added his own dramatic touch in many places. The tragic character of Coriolanus is a balance between a valiant warrior who was wounded defending Rome against the Volscians, and his unwillingness to pander to the masses in order to win their popularity. In one scene, several citizens of Rome come to meet him as he is being considered for the office of consul. They acknowledge his victory over their enemies, but remind him "you have not indeed loved the common people" (Act 2, Scene 3, lines 97 -98; 55.) He responds, "You should account me the more virtuous that I have not been common in my love" (Lines 99-100). At their urging he agrees to flatter the people, but after the citizens leave, he changes his mind, stating he would rather forfeit the office and its honor; indeed, better even to die than fawn upon the masses to receive what his service to Rome has already earned.

Just as the uncontrolled temper of Achilles turned him against his own people, Coriolanus rejects Rome after being rejected, joins the Volscians and prepares to attack his owe people. Only the entreaties of his mother prevent him from doing so, and when the Volscians perceive his help is lost, they attack and kill him. Whether wrath or "grandeur" or some other form of pride, Lewis warns, it must be overcome by God's grace or the proud spirit will not yield in Heaven just as it refused to bend on earth.

Cowper (Ch 8, p34)

William Cowper (November 26, 1731–April 25, 1800) was born in Hertfordshire, England. Apprenticed to a lawyer, he trained for a career in law, but broke under the strain of preparing for the law examination. He was institutionalized for insanity, and during a life-long struggle with depression attempted suicide three times. Cowper turned to religion, wrote a hymn book with John Newton, a former slave trader and author of the song "Amazing Grace." He was a prolific writer of letters, hymns, poetry and even a translation of Homer's *Iliad* and *Odyssey*. Tragically, his religious devoutness did not free him from doubts of his salvation and the belief that he was destined for Hell.

Lewis found Cowper to his liking. In a letter to his father, he described him as having

> ...nothing—literally nothing—to tell any one about... and yet one reads a whole volume of his correspondence with unfailing interest. How his tooth came loose at dinner, how he made a hutch for a tame hare, what he is doing about his cucumbers—all this he

makes one follow as if the fate of empires hung on it ("To His Father," February 25, 1928; CLI: 747-748).

Cowper often referred to his eye problems and his severe depression in his correspondence, and the quotation Lewis gives ("These are the sharpest arrows in His quiver") comes from a letter that well illustrates the feeling of condemnation that resulted from the melancholy that afflicted Cowper. The opening paragraph of that letter reads:

Dear Sir:

`Nothing new has occurred in my experience since we saw you, one circumstance excepted of the distressing kind. I have often told you that the notices given to you come to me unattended by any sensible effort; yet believing that they are from God, and gracious answers to your prayers, I have been accustomed to lean a little upon them, and have been the better able to sustain the constant pressure of my burthens. But of late I have been totally deprived of even that support, having been assured that though they are indeed from God, so far from being designed as comforts to me, to me they are reproaches, biting sarcasms, sharp strokes of irony,—in short, the deadliest arrows to be found in the quiver of the Almighty. To you indeed they are manna, and to Mrs. Unwin, because you are both at peace with God; but to me, who have unpardonably offended Him, they are a cup of deadly wine, against which there is no antidote. So the cloudy pillar was light to Israel, but darkness and horror to Egypt. ("Letter to Samuel Teedon," January 25, 1793; Cowper, *Correspondence*: 360-361)

Dog in a Manger (Ch 13, p 63)

"The Dog in the Manger" is one of Aesop's fables. An ox rebukes a dog who has found a manger to be an ideal resting place. Not wanting to be disturbed, it snarls whenever the ox approaches. It doesn't want to eat the straw and won't let the ox eat it either. Moral: some begrudge others what they cannot themselves enjoy.

Also, the same idea appears in the Gospel of Thomas. Logion (Saying) 102, which may be a genuine saying of Jesus not recorded in the canonical gospels, reads:

Jesus said: "Woe to the Pharisees! For they are like a dog lying in the manger of oxen; for he neither eats nor lets the oxen eat." (*Synopsis*: 529)

This proverb takes on tremendous significance in the final dialogue between Lewis and his tour guide. Because the only people who will suffer in Hell are those who choose to be there, there is no need to feel compassion for them. They have what they wanted. Heaven was ready to welcome them, but only on Heaven's terms—the removal of all sin and the transformation of the natural into the spiritual. If people were sent to Hell by God because they weren't chosen by him, or because they (through no fault of their own) never heard of redemption through Christ, then compassion would be in order and the justice of God would be lacking. Since this is not the case, those who do not want Heaven (as the dog did not want to eat straw) will not prevent those who do want Heaven from enjoying it.

Eastern Windows (Ch 2, p 21)

The Episcopal Ghost was quoting from the poem "Say Not the Struggle Naught Availeth" by Arthur Hugh Clough (January 1, 1819—November 13, 1861) to support his conviction that dawn, not night, would soon break upon the grey town. The complete poem reads:

> Say not the struggle naught availeth,
>   The labour and the wounds are vain,
> The enemy faints not, nor faileth,
>   And as things have been, they remain.
>
> If hopes were dupes, fears may be liars;
>   It may be, in yon smoke conceal'd,
> Your comrades chase e'en now the fliers,
>   And, but for you, possess the field.
>
> For while the tired waves, vainly breaking,
>   Seem here no painful inch to gain,
> Far back, through creeks and inlets making,
>   Comes silent, flooding in, the main.
>
> And not by eastern windows only,
>   When daylight comes, comes in the light;
> In front the sun climbs slow, how slowly,
>   But westward, look, the land is bright.
> (Clough, *Poems*: 345)

Clough, a Victorian poet and close friend of Matthew Arnold, won a scholarship to Balliol college, Oxford, at the age of fourteen. He struggled during his brief life to reconcile traditional Anglican theology with the new advances of science, such as evolution, and German higher criticism. The above poem expresses the sentiment of fighting the good fight of faith as he struggled with his "doubt about the relation between man, God, and the world" (Harris: 8).

Enemy (p 41)

A reference to Satan. Lewis did not refer to Satan in *The Great Divorce* because he intended to focus upon the importance of human choice in the process of sanctification, and Heaven's response to that choice. One might get the impression from this book that Lewis did not attach very much importance to the activity of Satan on earth. But that would be far from the truth; only a few years earlier, in *The Screwtape Letters*, Lewis described the human drama from the diabolical perspective. Both perspectives are needed in order for the full picture to emerge.

And that full picture is ... warfare. Nations at war describe their foes as "the enemy" and it is worth noting that both books were written during the greatest war this world has seen. But there is an even greater war raging, according to the Bible, and human souls are at stake. To pass over this fact is to fail to understand Lewis. All humanity, he was convinced, like it or not, realize it or not, is involved in a very long and fierce battle. And so, from the human perspective, Satan is the enemy. But from Screwtape's perspective, God is the enemy. In fact, Lewis referred to God as the "Enemy" one hundred and forty-nine times in Screwtape's thirty-one letters, and another nine times in his "Toast," for a total of one hundred and fifty-eight times (Clark: 25).

Lewis revealed his perspective on this warfare in many passages, such as this reflection on prayer that is not always answered.

> ...Little people like you and me, if our prayers are sometimes granted, beyond all hope and probability, had better not draw hasty conclusions to our own advantage. If we were stronger, we might be less tenderly treated. If we were braver, we might be sent, with far less help, to defend far more desperate posts in the great battle ("The Efficacy of Prayer," in WLN: 10-11).

Golden Apples/Garden of the Hesperides (Ch 6, p 31)

Lewis provides no clue as to the significance of this tree, but he is surely drawing upon the rich background of golden apples from a variety of sources. Dante, a primary source for Lewis, includes golden trees within the landscape of the earthly paradise at the top of the mountain of Purgatory:

> Seven golden trees a little way before us
> We seemed to see, though, truly, the long tract
> 'Twixt us and them cast this delusion o'er us.
> (*Purgatory*, Canto xxix. 43-45: 299)

Turning to Greek mythology, the eleventh of the twelve tasks given to Heracles (Hercules) was to find the Garden of the Hesperides (nymphs of the evening) and bring back from there three golden apples. Gaia (the earth mother) had given golden apples conferring immortality to Zeus and Hera as a wedding gift, and Hera had planted them in her garden. After many trials Heracles succeeded, but the apples were eventually returned to the garden where they belonged.

This garden from Greek mythology is lovingly mentioned by Milton in *Comus*, a poem Lewis knew very well.

> To the Ocean now I fly,
> And those happy climes that lie
> Where day never shuts his eye,
> Up in the broad fields of the sky:
> There I suck the liquid air
> All amidst the Gardens fair
> Of *Hesperus*, and his daughters three
> That sing about the golden tree:
> (*Comus:* lines 976-982: 113)

Milton is describing in his imagination a spirit visiting the Gardens of the Hesperides, located in the True Earth, far to the West, beside the river Oceanus that circles the earth. There, Venus and Adonis are found, and in another region reside Cupid and Psyche, her labors done, now eternally married. She will give birth to twins: Youth and Joy. It's worth noting that Lewis had Ransom quote lines 977-979 as he marveled at the beauty of space on his way to Mars (SP: 32), and that the marriage of Cupid and Psyche is the subject of his book *Till We Have Faces*.

Lewis explains Milton's spirit as one of the "aerial daemons" that live in the atmosphere, below the aetherial beings who live in what we would call space. The belief was that the Spirit of Nature would send forth gardens and orchards of delightful fruits into the air. The Hesperian Garden was mistakenly located in myth beyond the ocean at the end of the earth (CLIII, "To the Editor of the *Times Literary Supplement*," July 14, 1945; 1560-1).

As for the apples themselves, when thanking Ruth Pitter for a gift of marmalade, he traced that word back "thro' Portuguese from *Meli-mela*, 'honey-apples' which was what the benighted Greeks called oranges, and oranges might be the golden apples of the Western garden" (CLIII, "To Ruth Pitter," March 5, 1955; 577).

One of the more famous myths involving a golden apple describes the wedding of Peleus and Thetis, the parents of Achilles. Eris (goddess of discord) was not invited, so in her anger she threw down a golden apple with the inscription that it was meant for the most beautiful. Three goddesses claimed it; Athena, Hera and Aphrodite. Paris, the son of Priam, King of Troy, was chosen to decide between the three and he selected Aphrodite, since she had bribed him with the promise of Helen, the most beautiful woman in the world, and the wife of Menelaus of Sparta. Upon the advice of Aphrodite, Paris built ships, sailed to Sparta, and carried off Helen. This injustice led to the Trojan War, and Helen became known as the face that launched a thousand ships.

A third garden, this time in Genesis, may also lie behind this tree with golden apples. The tree of the knowledge of good and evil may not have been an apple tree, though it is often described as such in Christian tradition. Lewis chose to think of it in that way, probably viewing it as akin to the pagan myths.

> The story in Genesis is a story... about a magic apple of knowledge; but in the developed doctrine the inherent magic of the apple has quite dropped out of sight, and the story is simply one of disobedience. I have the deepest respect even for Pagan myths, still more for myths in the Holy Scriptures. I therefore do not doubt that the version which emphasizes the magic apple, and brings together the trees of life and knowledge, contains a deeper and subtler truth than the version which makes the apple simply and solely a pledge of disobedience (PP: 71-72).

These apples from various traditions may well have influenced Lewis when he described the beginnings of Narnian history. Digory's mother is very ill, and he knows one of the silver apples will heal her. (Narnia is not the true Heaven, and so the apples are silver, not gold.) Jadis the Witch urges him to take the apple to her, but with tremendous effort, he resists the desire to make his mother whole again, and takes the apple to Aslan instead. He instructs Digory to throw it into the mud near the river, where it will grow into a tree that will protect all of Narnia.

And what if Digory had brought the apple to his mother instead? "It would have healed her," Aslan explains, "but not to your joy or hers. The day would have come when both you and she would have looked back and said it would have been better to die in that illness" (MN: 175). Obedience is always the best policy. "If only," we can hear Lewis say in his heart, "if only there had been such an apple for my mother."

In sum, golden apples represent for Lewis, as in mythology, the promise of immortality. In the Christian context, immortality is also associated with a tree; the tree of life (and the water of life) which will be part of the restoration of all things (Rev 22:1-2). God will invite his people to partake of the trees of life ("Blessed are those who wash their robes, so that they will have the right to the tree of life and may enter the city by the gates and the water of life Revelation 22:14), and to drink ("let everyone who is thirsty come" Rev 22:17).

Also, such apples are to be found not in isolation but in a garden. The story of God and humanity begins in a garden and will also end there, according to the Scriptures. "The enclosed garden with its silver and golden fruit, heavenly scent, and golden gates, perched on top of a hill or mountain is the garden of the human soul, the church, and the real heavenly abode of all Christians who received salvation" (Khoddam, 9).

Lewis thus found in both pagan and Christian sources imagery associated with gardens, and in the midst of them trees that promised, someday, divine nature to humans. Reflecting upon what Heaven will be like, and recalling the mythological wedding of Peleus and Thetis that led to the Trojan war, Lewis wrote:

> The golden apple of selfhood, thrown among the false gods, became an apple of discord because they scrambled for it. They did not know the first rule of the holy game, which is that every player must by all means touch the ball and then immediately pass it on... When it flies to and fro among the players too swift for eye to follow, and the great master Himself leads the revelry, giving Himself eternally to His creatures in the generation, and back to Himself in the sacrifice, of the Word, then indeed the eternal dance "makes Heaven drowsy with the harmony" (PP: 153).

Ikey wanted to take the "golden apple of selfhood" back down to the souls in the grey town, but it was much too real for those in flight from reality. The bright angel in the waterfall invited him to stay and grow in selfhood until he could eat such apples, but Ikey ignored the invitation to participate in the divine nature (GD: 51).

Golders Green (Ch 12, p 57)

Golders Green is an actual place. It's been part of the parish of Hendon since the 13th century, and is now a cosmopolitan district of London, in the Borough of Barnet, known for a prominent Jewish community.

Golders Green is particularly noted for its crematorium; the first in London, and the "flagship" of crematoriums around the world. There are beautiful buildings on grounds of twelve landscaped acres, including even a children's section. Many famous people have been cremated there, including Sigmund Freud, H. G. Wells, Alice Liddell (for whom *Alice in Wonderland* was written), Rudyard Kipling, T. S. Eliot and Sir Kingsley William Amis (April 16, 1922–October 22, 1995) who had personal contact with Lewis. "Unreal Estates" is a conversation between Lewis, Amis and Brian Aldiss on the subject of science fiction (*Of Other Worlds*: 86-96).

Henry the Fifth (Ch 2, p 21)

The oldest son of Henry IV, at the age of fourteen he was already an accomplished warrior. After fighting with the Welsh, he invaded France to recapture the lands of Normandy and Anjou, once in English possession, thus reopening the Hundred Years War. Perhaps this is the reason Lewis included his name among those in Hell, though Henry sincerely believed he had the right to claim those lands.

His defeat of the French at Agincourt in 1415 is one of the most famous English victories. Claiming the French throne, he married Catherine, daughter of the French king Charles VI in 1420 and the future king Henry VI, was born to them in 1421, their only son.. Prematurely aged by invading France three times, he became ill and died in 1422 without ever having seen his son. Historians describe him as a man of virtues and noble qualities and that as an effective ruler, he was steadfast in purpose, though ruthless at times with his enemies.

Lewis probably singled out this British monarch (1387-1422) for the same reason he chose Tamberlaine; he was made famous in a play. *The Life of Henry the Fifth* by William Shakespeare was written in 1599 and describes Henry's ambitious conquest of France. The only indictment from Shakespeare is that he is "warlike" (*The Life of Henry the Fifth*, Prologue, line 5: 39). Lewis noted in his diary that he read this play in 1922, and found it disagreeable at first, because the king was "a most inexcusable war lord." But Shakespeare evidently left his mark on Lewis; before he was finished reading the play, he was "quite converted" (AMR: 144).

Henry VIII (Ch 7)

The second son of Henry VII and Elizabeth of York (1491-1547). His capable reign is often overshadowed by his search for a successor that took him through six marriages until finally Jane Seymour was able to bear him a son. Lewis disapproved of both his disregard for the sanctity of marriage, and his lack of respect for the Christian faith. In his dialogue with an Italian priest, Lewis wrote: "That the whole cause of schism lies in sin I do not hold to be certain. I grant that no schism is without sin but the one proposition does necessarily follow the other. From your side Tetzel, from ours Henry VIII, were lost men..." (CLII, "To Don Giovanni Calabria," November 25, 1947; 815).

Lewis explains himself further when he discusses both men in his introduction to *English Literature in the Sixteenth Century*, the volume he contributed to the *Oxford History of English Literature* series. The selling of indulgences, Lewis believed, might not have stirred up so much trouble if

Tetzel had not used "grotesquely profane and vulgar means of salesmanship." As for Henry, wanting Anne Boleyn, he quarreled with the pope and, though he cared nothing for Protestant doctrine, he accidentally created "a situation in which Protestantism, sometimes exploited and sometimes repressed by government, can become important in England" (EL: 37-38).

Josephine (Ch 2, p 21)

Marie-Rose de Tascher de la Pagerie (1763-1814) was born in the West Indies to a family that was not wealthy but she did marry into nobility. Napoleon met Rose at a party, and was smitten by her charms. She found him to be a bore, but needed the financial security he could provide, In turn, he needed an older wife, since he had become a general at such a young age. Her social skills and political connections helped Napoleon rise to power. He didn't like the name Marie-Rose and decided to call her Josephine. Their marriage was tumultuous; she was unfaithful to him while he was away on military campaigns, and he was furious when he found out. He eventually divorced her, and had many affairs with other women, but she remained true to him until her death.

Julian, Lady (Ch 13, p xix)

Julian of Norwich (c. 1342-after 1411) was an English mystic. Not much is known of her life, but she claimed to have received a series of fifteen revelations on May 8, 1373 in a state of ecstasy that lasted some sixteen hours. One more revelation came the next day, and after reflecting for some twenty years upon the meaning of these visions of the Trinity and the Passion of Christ, she published *The Sixteen Revelations of Divine Love*.

In regard to the question that vexed Lewis, she believed that in the thirteenth revelation God revealed to her the following truths:

1. Even the smallest, most lowly and humble things will not be forgotten by God. All shall be well.

2. Our human reason is not able to grasp the wisdom of God, and so the effects of sin seem to us to be impossible to overcome.

3. On the last day, God will accomplish a "grand deed" that will make all things well. He will not reveal what this deed will be to anyone now, but gives us the reassurance that he will indeed make all things well.

4. He gives us this assurance so that we can trust him more fully and be at more ease in our souls.

5. We should become more like the saints now in heaven, who desire to know only what God wishes them to know.

The Great Divorce is the "dream" where Lewis pondered this promise of universalism and found the answer not in the salvation of every soul, but in each soul obtaining what it wished. Will this be the "grand deed?" The answer will not come in this world, MacDonald tells Lewis (and so Lewis tells his readers); the important thing is the freedom each soul has now to choose between Heaven and Hell, (GD: 122).

Julius Caesar (Ch 2, p 9)

Gaius Julius (July 13, 100 - March 15, 44 BCE) was a famous statesman and author who conquered Gaul (France and Belgium) and changed Rome from a republic to a monarchy by overriding the Senate, becoming the first Caesar (a dictator) and amassing many honors to himself. He was assassinated by a group of senators, led by Brutus and Cassius, on the Ides of March. In 42, he was formally deified as "the divine Julius."

Lewis met Julius Caesar both in his classics studies and on the stage. He was not the most enthusiastic supporter of Shakespeare, but did appreciate his play *Julius Caesar*. "Although I do not join with Warnie in condemning Shakespeare, I must say that in a good many plays he has missed alike the realism of modern plays and the statliness (sic) of Greek tragedies. Julius Caesar is one of his best in some ways ("Letter to His Father," January 6, 1913; CLI: 22).

In the play, Caesar yields to his wife's pleas not to go to the Capitol on the fateful day (he had been warned), but changes his mind after Decius, one of the plotters, shames him out of his cowardice. Does he expect the people to crown him, Decius asks, when he fails to appear because he is afraid to come? Caesar resolves to go, as Decius hopes he would, and so walks into the trap his assassins have laid for him. In the end, his ambition for power replaced the republican form of Roman government with a dictatorship, and his pride led to his murder by senators who were concerned for Rome's future.

Khan, Genghis (Ch 2, p 9)

Perhaps the most famous Mongol ruler. Characterized by ambition and cruelty, Khan (1162-1227) united the Mongol tribes and so founded the Mongolian empire that at its peak, ruled more contiguous territory than any other empire in history.

Keats (Ch 11, p 52)

John Keats (October 31, 1795 - February 23, 1821); now recognized as one of the greatest English poets.

Lewis asked MacDonald about the Romantic poet's view of the human heart. Keats had written: "I am certain of nothing but the holiness of the Heart's affections and the truth of Imagination—what the imagination seizes as Beauty must be truth—whether it existed before or not - for I have the same idea of all our passions as of love: they are all, in their sublime, creative of essential beauty." (*Complete Poetical Works*; "Letter to Benjamin Bailey," November 22, 1817: 274.)

After describing Pam's insistence that God restore her son Michael to her, Lewis cautions the reader against Keats' high opinion of the natural loves, and charitably suggests that Keats may not have fully understood what he had written about the holiness of the heart's affections. Only when the natural affections are put to death by God can they rise again and become what they are meant to be. "There is but one good; that is God. Everything else is good when it looks to Him and bad when it turns from Him. And the higher and mightier it is in the natural order, the more demoniac it will be if it rebels"(96).

Lethe (Ch 9, p 46)

River of the earthly Paradise. Dante asks where Lethe is and Virgil tells him:

> And Lethe thou shalt see, far from this pit,
> Where the souls go to wash them in its flood,
> Their guilt purged off, their penance complete.
> (*Hell*, XIV. 136-138, p. 160).

As they climb out of Hell, they follow the river Lethe up to Purgatory. When they reach the earthly Paradise at the top of Mount Purgatory, Dante sees water from two fountains welling up: Lethe the river of forgetfulness in Greek mythology, and Eunoe, the river of Good Remembrance. First the souls must drink from Lethe to forget the memory of evil and the sin that created it; then from Eunoe to restore the memory of sin, but only as a historical fact and the occasion of grace and God's redemption.

> This water that thou see'st wells from no spring
> By condensation of cold cloud supplied,
> Like streams that have their spate and slackening,
>
> But from a fount whose sure and constant tide
> Ever by God's good will regains at source
> Whate'er it freely spends on either side.

With twofold powers it runs a twofold course:
> This side blots all man's sins from memory;
> That side to memory all good deeds restores;

Lethe this side, and that side Eunoe
> We name it; and to make its work complete
> This must be tasted first; that secondly;

Lo there a taste beyond all savours sweet!
>   (*Purgatory*, Canto xxviii. 121-133: 292)

There are similar Biblical traditions; God will restore the tree of life that was in Paradise (see the Golden Apples entry) and there will be a river of the water of life in the new Jerusalem (Rev 22:1-2). There is even a promise that in the restoration of all things, humans will experience a merciful forgetting of the past, though this forgetting is not specifically associated with the river of life. Isaiah prophesied: "For I am about to create new heavens and a new earth; the former things shall not be remembered or come to mind" (Isa 65:17 NRSV)

MacDonald, George (Ch 9, p 1)

Lewis discovered the Scottish minister and author (1824-1905) quite by accident when he read *Phantastes* in 1916. His excitement is palpable as he writes to Arthur Greeves, telling him "I have had a great literary experience this week... whatever book you are reading now, you simply MUST get this at once" (CLI, "To Arthur Greeves," March 7, 1916; 169-170).

Seven years later, he had reread it several times and felt it had become a devotional book for him. "It tuned me up to a higher pitch and delighted me" (AMR, January 11, 1923; 177). In another letter he describes the book as "endlessly attractive, and full of what I felt to be holiness before I really knew that it was" (CLII, "To Sister Penelope," August 9, 1939; 263).

Later still, he was able to explain his "great literary experience" as a baptism of his imagination during a time when he was under the sway of Romanticism and in danger of yielding to strangeness, then eccentricity and finally perversity. MacDonald's antidote was to return Lewis to the real world, since "the quality which had enchanted me in his imaginative works turned out to be the quality of the real universe" (*George MacDonald: An Anthology*, xxxiv).

MacDonald had a reputation of being a universalist. He believed that God's love for humanity meant that the fires of Hell were not intended as unending punishment but serve the redemptive purpose of eventually bringing the sinner to the realization of his need for God. His theology of universalism made him unpopular in the pulpits of his Congregational churches, and he and his family experienced financial hardships as a result. Despite a life of poverty, he remained cheerful, finding work where he could and also finding time to write more than forty books, plus many poems and sermons.

Mermaid (Ch 9, p xix)

Hans Christian Andersen (1805-1875) wrote the story of "The Little Mermaid" in 1836. She fell in love with a prince and wanted to become a human to marry him. The witch at the bottom of the sea gave her a potion to do this, but in exchange she wanted the mermaid's tongue. And she would have human legs instead of a tail, but each step would be as painful as walking on knives. The mermaid accepted these terms and suffered greatly with each step. Unable to speak her love, she could not prevent the prince from marrying someone else. But the daughters of Heaven took her to be with them, promising that after three hundred years of good deeds, she would receive an immortal soul.

Milton (Ch 9, p xix)

John Milton (December 9, 1608-1674) was born in London, schooled in classical languages at home and then in St. Paul's School from the age of 12. Attended Christ's College at Cambridge, from 1625 -1632, leaving with an M. A. degree. A prolific writer for political causes, he lost his sight to glaucoma in 1652, but continued writing. He would compose the lines of his masterpieces *Paradise Lost* and *Paradise Regained* in his mind at night, and then dictate them to his assistants during the day. He is regarded as one of the greatest poets of the English language.

These are the words of Satan in context in Milton's *Paradise Lost*, Chapter One:

> Here we may reign secure; and, in my choice,
> To reign is worth ambition, though in Hell:
> Better to reign in Hell than serve in Heaven.

Few humans would compare their own lives to that of Satan, or even want to. But Lewis held that whether great or small, sins must be removed. To refuse God's grace is to put self above God's will and so join Satan's rebellion.

Monet (Ch 9, p 46)

Claude Monet, Nov. 14, 1840 - Dec 5, 1926, prolific French painter and founder of the Impressionist style. Friend and associate of Sargent, Monet's work has earned high praise indeed. "Avoiding dry, detailed empiricism by strong brushwork, he came closer to perceptual reality than has anyone else" (Seitz: 10).

Moore, Janie (p 19)

Janie King ("Minto") Moore (1872-1951), the woman who depended upon Lewis for many years. She was married to Courtenay Edward Moore in 1897 and they had two children: Edward Francis Courtenay, or "Paddy," and Maureen Daisy Helen. After Janie separated from her husband, she moved to Bristol where her brother was a doctor. Paddy joined the Officer's Training Corps in 1917 and was sent to Keble College, Oxford, where he met Lewis and the two young men became fast friends.

During that same year, Lewis met Janie, and they got along well. Shortly before Paddy and Lewis were sent to the front, they each promised to look after the other's parent should one of them not survive. Paddy was reported missing on March, 1918, and his death confirmed in April.

Lewis made good on his promise; Janie moved in with Lewis in 1919, and lived with him until her death. Lewis greatly benefitted from the home life she provided, though for most of her life she was an atheist and chided Lewis and his brother for attending church services (Hooper, *C. S. Lewis, Companion and Guide*, 712-715).

Napoleon (Ch 2, p 9)

Born Napoleone di Buonaparte in Corsica on August 15, 1769 into a family of minor nobility, he later changed his name to the more French-sounding Napoleon Bonaparte. At the age of nine, he began study at a French military school, where he showed aptitude for mathematics and geography. Admitted to the elite Ecole Royale Militaire in Paris at the age of 14, he complete the two year course of study in just one, and began active duty as a second lieutenant of artillery at the age of 16.

Over the course of some ten years, he led the French army against nearly every European country, and eventually controlled most of western and central Europe. His invasion of Russia, however, proved disastrous. His losses there encouraged European powers to unite against him and he lost many troops at Leipzig in 1813. Sensing inevitable defeat he abdicated and was sent into exile on the island of Elba. He escaped from Elba in 1815 and attempted to regain power. After ruling for 100 days, the Duke of Wellington defeated him in the battle of Waterloo, and he was again exiled, this time to the island of Saint Helena where he died on May 5, 1821.

He was a brilliant strategist and modernized the French army. His battles are still studied today, and the Duke of Wellington regarded him as the greatest general of all time. But Lewis sees him as just another ruthless person who conquered many others but himself was conquered by his own ambition and pride.

Neo-Regionalists (p 81)

The Neo-Regionalists who sent the Artist Ghost into obscurity belonged to a period of art, literature, architecture, etc. which was, as its name implies, a return to Regionalism. Regionalism in turn was the school that preferred the realistic depiction of rural settings over urban scenes. Neo-Regionalism was especially strong in America during the depression of the 1930's. For Lewis, the realistic depiction of nature, or Regionalism, was an opportunity for the artist to give the viewer glimpses of the Creator's handiwork, while abstract art replaced that in favor of the expression of the moods and viewpoints of the artist. Since the artist wanted to meet Monet and Cezanne, his style was no doubt influenced by them. Forsaking modern art would mean for Lewis portraying nature (especially light) as it reflects God, and relinquishing the focus upon self and reputation.

Ney (Ch 2, p 21)

Michel Ney (1769-1815) was one of the Napoleonic War's generals, much loved by his soldiers and regarded by Napoleon as "the bravest of the brave." After the setbacks at Leipzig and Paris, Ney approached Napoleon and urged him to abdicate. Louis XVIII allowed Ney to retain his position and rank for this, and after Napoleon escaped from Elba, sent him to bring Napoleon back. Ney promised to do so, but changed his mind and once again went to battle with Napoleon. After the defeat of Waterloo, he was brought to trial, found guilty of returning to Napoleon, and executed by firing squad.

Owens, Vale (Ch 14, p 85)

The plural of Owen, namely George Vale Owen. Rev. Vale (1869- 1931) was born in Birmingham, England, and educated at the Midland Institute and Queen's College in that city. He was ordained by the bishop of Liverpool to the curacy of Seaforth in 1893; then was curate successively of Fairfield, 1895, and of Matthew's, Scotland Road, 1897—both of Liverpool. In 1900 he moved to Orford, Warrington, as curate-in-charge where he began giving his famous readings, eventually published by him in *The Life Behind the Veil*. (These details of Owen's life are taken from the "Appreciation" by Lord Northcliffe in *The Veil*, p. 6.)

His *Life Beyond the Veil* contains five books: The Lowlands of Heaven, The Highlands of Heaven, The Ministry of Heaven, The Battalions of Heaven, and The Outlands of Heaven.

C. S. Lewis Goes to Heaven

Owen claimed that for many years he was quite reluctant to believe in communications from the spirit world, and even less willing to be a channel for messages from spirit beings:

> There is an opinion abroad that the clergy are very credulous beings. But our training in the exercise of the critical faculty places us among the most hard-to-convince when any new truth is in question. It took a quarter of a century to convince me—ten years that spirit communication was a fact, and fifteen that the fact was legitimate and good.

> From the moment I had taken this decision, the answer began to appear. First my wife developed the power of automatic writing. Then through her I received requests that I would sit quietly, pencil in hand, and take down any thoughts which seem to come into my mind projected there by some external personality and not consequent on the exercise of my own mentality. Reluctance lasted a long time, but at last I felt that friends were at hand who wished very earnestly to speak with me. They did not overrule or compel my will in any way—that would have settled the matter at once, so far as I was concerned—but their wishes were made ever more plain.

> I felt at last that I ought to give them an opportunity, for I was impressed with the feeling that the influence was a good one, so, at last, very doubtfully I decided to sit in my cassock in the vestry after Evensong.

> The first four or five messages wandered aimlessly from one subject to another. But gradually the sentences began to take consecutive form, and at last I got some which were understandable. From that time, development kept pace with practice. When the whole series of messages was finished I reckoned up and found that the speed had been maintained at an average rate of twenty-four words a minute. On two occasions only had I any idea what subject was to be treated. That was when the message had obviously been left uncompleted. At other times I had fully expected a certain subject to be taken, but on taking up my pencil the stream of thought went off in an altogether different direction. ("Lowlands of Heaven:" 9)

Here is a brief summary of the spirit world as revealed to Owen by the ascended beings:

Life is much similar to life on earth, but there are higher levels of Heaven that must be gradually ascended. Higher beings (visible if they choose to be) come down to help those on lower levels. But first they must become accustomed to the dimmer light and murky air of the lower spheres; a process that changes them and often renders their messages difficult to receive. The teachings from them are many and complex, but they seem to include universalism (all eventually will be saved), and a rejection of Christianity's understanding of Christ, who is actually less than God the Father. This misunderstanding of Christ on the earth is beyond repair, so angels are guiding the dismantling of this theology so it can eventually be replaced by the truth. Mars is inhabited. There is a Hell, a place of deep mines and slavery, but help is given to everyone when they are ready. Those who die are helped into the next world by the spirits; they go to the sphere that corresponds to the level of spirituality they reached before death.

The similarities between Lewis' Heaven and that of Owen are remarkable indeed. Both use the landscapes of earth to describe Heaven, both have lower and higher levels, and both describe beings from higher levels coming down to assist the spiritual progress of souls dwelling on lower levels. But, unlike Owen, Lewis insists his descriptions of Heaven must not be taken literally. And Lewis would also insist that Christ is fully divine and the only source of salvation.

Commenting on the significance of Owen's communications, Sir Arthur Conan Doyle (Sir Archibald in GD) writes:

How many fleeting phrases of the old Scriptures now take visible shape and meaning? Do we not begin to understand that "House with many mansions," and realize Paul's "House not made with hands," even as we catch some fleeting glance of that glory which the mind of man has not conceived, neither has his tongue spoken.

It all ceases to be a far-off elusive vision and it becomes real, solid, assured, a bright light ahead as we sail the dark waters of Time, adding a deeper joy to our hours of gladness and wiping away the tear of sorrow by assuring us that if we are only true to God's law and our own higher instincts there are no words to express the happiness which awaits us. ("Lowlands of Heaven:" 14-15)

In answer to Owen's question of what life is like in Heaven's lowlands, the spirit Astriel says:

Earth made perfect. But of course what you call a fourth dimension does exist here, in a way, and that hinders us in describing it adequately. We have hills and rivers and beautiful forests, and houses, too, and all the work of those who have come before us to make ready. We are at present at work, in our turn, building and ordering for those who must still for a little while continue their battle on earth, and when they come they will find all things ready and the feast prepared. ("Lowlands of Heaven:" 18)

Paradise (p xv)

Origin uncertain; probably from the Persian "pardes" where it meant a royal park or orchard. The word is used only three times in the New Testament, where it means the place in the spirit world for those who belong to God. On the cross, Jesus promised the thief "today you will be with me in Paradise" (Luke 23:43). Later, Paul claimed that he was caught up to the third heaven and entered Paradise, where he heard words impossible (or forbidden) to express (2 Cor 12:4). And one of the promises to believers who remain faithful is access to the tree of life which is "in the Paradise of God" (Rev 2:7).

When Jesus was preparing his disciples for his departure, he promised to make a change in the spirit world for them: "In my Father's house there are many dwelling places. If it were not so, would I have told you that I go to prepare a place for you? And if I go and prepare a place for you, I will come again and will take you to myself, so that where I am, there you may be also" (John 14:2-3). I conclude from this passage that the place Jesus prepared was the Paradise to which Paul was caught up; surely he would deserve as much as the thief on the cross. The words of Jesus imply that the spirit world did not have a suitable place for the followers of Jesus, and Lewis also came to this conclusion as he pondered this passage. "This presumably means that He is about to create that whole new Nature which will provide the environment or conditions for His glorified humanity and, in Him, for ours" (M: 154). (Verify quotation)

Note: in the Latin (Vulgate) and Greek (Septuagint) versions of the Old Testament, the word "Paradise" is used instead of "garden" in reference to the Garden of Eden (Gen 2:9, 15, 16; 3:1. etc.) So then, when God prepares a place for humanity in the physical world, and then another place in the spirit world, they are both referred to as Paradises. Influenced by the Bible, Dante used Paradise as the title for the third volume of his *Comedy*, which features his vision of Heaven. Lewis, recalling Psa 23:4 ("Even though I walk through the valley of the shadow of death"), referred to his Paradise as "The Valley of the Shadow of Life" (67).

Phantastes (Ch 9, p 7)

The fairy romance by George MacDonald that made such a strong impression upon the pre-Christian Lewis. After passing by the bookstall several times, Lewis finally purchased the Everyman edition and began reading it. "A few hours later I knew that I had passed a great frontier." Reflecting back on this experience, he recalled that he was at that time well into Romanticism. *Phantastes* was certainly romantic but of a different kind, though at that time, Lewis did not realize exactly what was making such a deep impression upon him.

> I was only aware that if this new world was strange, it was also homely and humble, that if this was a dream, it was a dream in which one at least felt strangely vigilant, that the whole book had about it a sort of cool, morning innocence, and also, quite unmistakably, a certain quality of Death, *good* Death. What it actually did to me was to convert, even to baptise (sic) (that was where the Death came in) my imagination (Introduction to *George MacDonald: An Anthology*).

Even after Lewis became a mature Christian, MacDonald was still at his side, so to speak. "I found that I was still with MacDonald and that he had accompanied me all the way and that I was now at least ready to hear from him much that he could not have told me at that first meeting" (Introduction to *George MacDonald: An Anthology*).

Purgatory (Ch 9, p xi)

The place where the soul is purified after death. Dante envisioned his Purgatory as a mountain (some 3,000 miles high), with ten levels. At the top is the earthly Paradise from which man fell, empty now due to sin. If man had not fallen, his journey would begin here. Lewis simplifies Dante, omitting the ten levels and depicting the bus ride from the grey town ascending to a pastoral landscape resembling an earthly Paradise.

The grey town will be Purgatory for those who choose Heaven, and the outskirts of Heaven or Paradise will also be Purgatory for those who choose to stay. In the notes to her translation of Dante, Sayers explains how Dante's theology made the suffering of Hell and Purgatory so similar. Lewis used geography to follow Dante, making Purgatory simultaneously the outskirts of both Hell and Heaven.

> The pains of Purgatory are in themselves very like those of Hell, and some of them are but little lighter. ... The sole transforming difference is in the mental attitude of the sufferers. Dante has grasped the great essential which is so often overlooked in arguments about penal reform, namely, the prime necessity of persuading the culprit to accept judgment. If a man is once convinced of his own guilt, and that he is sentenced by a just tribunal, *all* punishment of whatever kind is remedial, since it lies with him to make it so; if he is not so convinced, then *all* punishment,

however enlightened, remains merely vindictive, since he sees it so and will not make it otherwise. ...the fire of Hell is simply the light of God as experienced by those who reject it; to those, that is, who hold fast to their darling illusion of sin, the burning reality of holiness is a thing unbearable. To the penitent, that reality is a torment so long and only so long as any vestige of illusion remains to hamper their assent to it: they welcome the torment, as a sick man welcomes the pains of surgery, in order that the last crippling illusion may be burned away. The whole operation of Purgatory is directed to the freeing of the judgement (sic) and the will (Sayers, *Purgatory*: 15-16)

The Roman Catholic view of Purgatory is the place where a believer who still has venial sin(s) goes so that forgivable sins can be removed. (Believers who have persevered in virtue and allowed God to accomplish their purgation in this life go directly into Heaven.) Also, even though God forgives sins, He requires punishment for them. If sins were not paid for on earth, souls suffer for them for a time in Purgatory. The condition of the soul and its purification is the essence of Purgatory in Catholic theology, not a certain place.

Catholics do not view Purgatory as a "second chance" for those who die refusing salvation. The choice between God and self made at death is final. Repentance at the moment of death (*in articulo mortis*) is always accepted by God. As long as the soul is moving away from self toward God, confession and contrition is complete and the soul will go to Purgatory. Once the cleansing of souls is complete, all in Purgatory will enter Heaven (Sayers, *Purgatory*: 59).

In Purgatory, although now accepted by God, the soul must, without the help of the body, with much labor and pain, accomplish the process of satisfaction and purification which should have been carried out on earth. In this context, prayer for the dead who are struggling with their sins makes as much sense as praying for those who are struggling with sin during their earthly lives. Catholics believe souls in Purgatory and believers on earth can aid each other by their prayers. But the living should not distract the dead from their task of purgation by demands for attention (Sayers, *Purgatory*: 60).

Lewis also found prayer for the dead an important part of his devotional life.

Of course I pray for the dead. The action is so spontaneous, so all but inevitable, that only the most compulsive theological case against it would deter me. And I hardly know how the rest of my prayers would survive if those for the dead were forbidden. At our age the majority of those we love best are dead. What sort of intercourse with God could I have if what I love best were unmentionable to Him (LTM: 107)?

Even those in Heaven, Lewis thought, might benefit from prayer. Though sin is no longer a problem there, "Even in Heaven some perpetual increase of beatitude, reached by a continually more ecstatic self-surrender, without the possibility of failure but not perhaps without its own ardours and exertions... might be supposed" (LTM: 108). Perhaps Dante's influence lies behind these words, for his Heaven has ten levels, and only with difficult spiritual growth and the help of Beatrice is he able to pass through all ten and attain for a brief time the vision of God himself.

The strength of both Roman Catholic theology and Lewis' theology lies in their emphasis upon the need for each soul to choose or reject God, and also that to choose God means being willing to accept any pain that the cleansing of the soul may bring. The importance of this view is that it vindicates the justice of God which many have attacked because they find the concept of Hell so objectionable. This emphasis upon choice found in both Dante and Lewis vindicates the justice of God. Sayers certainly speaks for Lewis when she writes:

> The accusation of cruelty, so often urged against the *Purgatorio* as well as against the *Inferno*, is therefore without meaning or relevance. Whether in Hell or Purgatory, you get what you want - if that is what you really do want. If you insist on having your own way, you will get it: Hell is the enjoyment of your own way for ever. If you really want God's way for you, you will get it in Heaven, and the pains of Purgatory will not deter you, they will be welcomed as the means to that end (Sayers, *Purgatory* 16).

Refrigerium (Prudentius): (Ch 9, p 3)

In his correspondence, Lewis wrote:

> About all I know of the "Refrigerium" is derived from Jeremy Taylor's sermon on "Christ's Advent to Judgement" and the quotations there given from a Roman missal printed at Paris in 1626, and from Prudentius. See Taylor's *Whole Works*, edit. R. Heber, London 1822, Vol. V: 45.

> The Prudentius says, "Often below the Styx holidays from their punishments are kept, even by the guilty spirits... Hell grows feeble with mitigated torments and the shadowy nation, free from fires, exults in the leisure of its prison; the rivers cease to burn with their usual sulphur." ("Letter to Henry Noel," November 14, 1962, in L: 505.)

As the quotation from Lewis shows and as Hooper clarifies, in addition to the Roman missal, Taylor also found another reference to the *Refrigerium* in the "Hymn for the Lighting of the Lamp" from the book *Liber Cathemerinon* by Aurelius Clemens Prudentius, a Christian poet from Northern Spain (348 - after 405). (Hooper, CSL: 279-280). The Latin word "Refrigerium" means a "cooling refreshment" and lies behind "refrigerator" in the English language.

Sarah Smith (Ch 9, p 29)

The first clue to the literary background of Sarah Smith is the quotation Lewis gives through MacDonald taken from Milton's *Comus:* "A thousand liveried angels lackey her." The quotation is very brief, but behind it lies a deep appreciation of Lewis for this poem by Milton. Lewis described it as "an absolute dream of delight... it is lovely in books the way you can just turn from one sort of beauty to another and never get tired" ("Letter to Arthur Greeves," September 27, 1916; CLI: 225). And in another letter to Arthur, Lewis viewed it as "one of the most perfect things in English poetry" (August 4, 1917; CLI: 332).

Milton personified virtues to better describe them in *Comus*; for example, Wisdom (personified as a woman), accompanied by her best nurse Contemplation, needs little protection; who would rob a Hermit of his few books? The same cannot be said of beauty.

> But beauty, like the fair Hesperian Tree
> Laden with blooming gold, had need the guard
> Of dragon wrath with unenchanted eye,
> To save her blossoms and defend her fruit
> From the rash hand of bold Incontinence.
> (*John Milton*, "Comus;" Lines 385-392: 99)

As for Chastity, the inspiration for Sarah;

> So dear to Heav'n is Saintly chastity,
> That when a soul is found sincerely so,
> A thousand liveried Angels lackey her,
> Driving far off each thing of sin and guilt,
> And in clear dream and solemn vision
> Tell her of things that no gross ear can hear,
> Till oft converse with heav'nly habitants
> Begin to cast a beam on th' outward shape,
> The unpolluted temple of the mind,
> And turns it by degrees to the soul's essence,
> Till all be made immortal:
> (*John Milton*, "Comus;" lines 453-463: 100-101)

Lewis certainly follows Milton here, making Sarah Smith, the image of "Saintly chastity," and impervious to every attempt of her husband to blackmail her with self-pity, thanks to her angelic bodyguard. She no longer needs him; every desire has been satisfied by Heaven. Now she can truly love him, which means desiring what is best for him. Heaven is best for him (and for everyone) and this he finally rejects. As for her, Heaven has "cast a beam" into the "temple of her mind" and all that she is has been "made immortal." The real Frank disappears even while the real Sarah stands before him.

But Milton provided no procession to escort chastity for her protection; Dante gets the credit for that. Lewis acknowledged his debt to Dante in his correspondence: "The unsuccessful meeting between the 'Tragedian' and his wife is a sort of pendant to the successful meeting of D. and Beatrice in the Earthly Paradise" (CLIII, "To William L. Kinter," July 30, 1954; 498).

When Dante's journey out of Purgatory brings him to realms of Heaven that the pagan Virgil cannot explain, a new tour guide must take his place. And so Dante introduces Beatrice, the great love of his life, by means of a beautiful procession. First he sees light:

> And lo! A flood of brilliance suddenly
> Through the great forest spread on every side,
>
> (*Purgatory*, Canto xxix. 16-17; 298)

Lewis announces the approach of Sarah Smith in the same manner: "All down one long aisle of the forest the under-sides of the leafy branches had begun to tremble with dancing light" (104).

Next Dante describes "a most dulcet melody" *Purgatory*, Canto xxix. 22) of a choir, then a procession of many spirit beings, hundreds of spirits, who comprise "The court and couriers of eternal life" (*Purgatory*, Canto 30, line 18; 307). Lewis agrees, producing his own procession of bright Spirits, "not the Spirits of men," and music beyond description.

Lewis asks "Who are these gigantic people… look! They're like emeralds… who are dancing and throwing flowers before her?" (105) MacDonald responds by quoting Milton ("A thousand liveried angels lackey her," (105) but the description is from Dante. One of the spirits in Beatrice's procession is clothed in emerald green:

> The next (woman) appeared of emerald through and through
> Both flesh and bone (*Purgatory*, Canto 29; Lines 124-125: 301)

Then Beatrice appears with flowers all around:

> So, even so, through cloud on cloud of flowers
> Flung from angelic hands and falling down
> Over the car and all around in showers,

In a white veil beneath an olive-crown
Appeared to me a lady cloaked in green,
And living flame the color of her gown.
(*Purgatory*, Canto 30; lines 28-33: 308)

As Beatrice was the means of spiritual grace to Dante, so Sarah is sent to her husband Frank to guide him into Heaven, but the last vestige of humor (the ability to laugh at oneself) disappears, a once-real personality is swallowed up by self-pity, and there is nothing left for Sarah to help.

Smoke of Hell (Ch 8, p 34)

Lewis is referring to the last book of the Bible, the Revelation of Jesus to John which he received while in exile on the Island of Patmos. Lewis is probably thinking of Ch. 14 which opens with a vision of the faithful rejoicing in Heaven, and then John records messages from three angels. The third angel warns:

> "Those who worship the beast and its image, and receive a mark on their foreheads or on their hands, [10] they will also drink the wine of God's wrath, poured unmixed into the cup of his anger, and they will be tormented with fire and sulfur in the presence of the holy angels and in the presence of the Lamb. [11] And the smoke of their torment goes up forever and ever. There is no rest day or night for those who worship the beast and its image and for anyone who receives the mark of its name." (Rev 14:9-11)

Soult (Ch 2, p 21)

Nicholas Jean de Dieu Soult, March 29, 1769 - November 26, 1851, one of Napoleon's generals, and also a Marshall of France. He was a brilliant strategist, but had a reputation for greediness.

Stable (p 113)

Lewis chose a stable in the last volume of the Narnian Chronicles to symbolize the spirit world because, as Lucy explained, "In our world too, a stable once had something inside it that was bigger than our whole world" (*The Last Battle, 140-141*). In fact, its inside was larger than its outside, just as the reality of Heaven is hard to grasp in this world that seems so solid. But once gained, Heaven will dwarf all that we once knew.

In his description of the final judgment of Narnia, Lewis is careful to note that Aslan stood where the door to the Stable would be on his right side. In this way, he was reflecting the Parable of The Sheep and the Goats (Matt 25:31-46); a parable that greatly interested Lewis. When Jesus comes to judge the nations, he will place the "sheep" (those who have been granted salvation) on his right side, but the goats on his left. Many cultures of that time (and even today) reflect a bias against the left hand. In Latin, for example, the word for left is *sinister.*

Swedenborg (es) (Ch 14, p 3)

The plural of Swedenborg. Emanuel von Swedenborg, 1688-1772, was a Swedish chemist, philosopher, theologian and mystic, among other things. His formal studies included mechanics, geography, astronomy and mathematics. In his fifties he began to have mystical experiences. These led him to devote himself to spiritual investigations. He claimed to have spoken to Christ, angels and spirits; to have seen Heaven and Hell, and to have taken a tour of the solar system. He rejected the atonement of Christ, believing that people make their own Heaven or Hell. The life of love for others is of foremost importance. He also rejected a literal return of Christ. Rather, the return of the spirit and truth of Christ to the church is the "Second Coming" and it is still continuing today.

Tacitus (Ch 9, p 44)

Cornelius Tacitus, Roman historian, c. A. D. 55- c. 117. He became a senator, rose to the rank of consul, and later became the governor of Asia (A. D. 112-113). His longer works describe imperial history from A. D. 14-96. The first, *Histories,* now survives only in four books and twenty-six chapters of a fifth. In addition, sixteen chapters of his *Annals* survive. His mastery of Latin has earned him the status of one of the greatest, if not the greatest, Roman stylists.

By 1917, Lewis could claim "I have read nearly all Tacitus… at first I absolutely hated him, partly because I had not then learned to appreciate history, partly because his twisted and obscure style… now, however, I am grown to be very fond of him indeed" ("To Arthur Greeves," February 28, 1917; CLI: 284)

Lewis probably took the quotation "They terrify lest they should fear" from Tacitus' *Germania,* Ch. 3, where he described German warriors preparing for battle.

> They also have the well-known kind of chant that they call *baritus.* By the rendering of this they not only kindle their courage, but, merely by listening to the sound, they can forecast the issue of an approaching engagement. For they either terrify their foes, or themselves become frightened (terrent enim trepidantue), according to the character of the noise they make upon the battlefield; and they regard it not merely as so many voices chanting together but as a unison of valour. What they particularly aim at is a harsh, intermittent roar, and they hold their

shields in front of their mouths, so that the sound is amplified into a deeper crescendo by the reverberation (*Tacitus on Britain and Germany*: 103).

Tamberlaine (Ch 2, p 21)

Also called Tamerlane or Timur Leng ("Timur the Lame"), a Mongol conqueror (c. 1336-1405) with a reputation for cruelty. He claimed to be a descendant of Genghis Khan. Lewis was quite familiar with this obscure tyrant through Christopher Marlowe, who wrote a famous two-part play on him, called *Tamburlaine the Great*, first published in 1590.

Marlowe wasted little time revealing the heart of the Scythian shepherd who had such grandiose plans. Upon meeting Theridamas, a Persian lord, early in the play, Tamburlaine invites him to join his cause:

> And we will triumph over all the world.
> I hold the Fates bound fast in yron chaines,
> And with my hand turne Fortunes wheel about,
> And sooner shall the Sun fall from his Spheare,
> Than Tamburlaine be slaine or overcome…
>
> If thou will stay with me, renowned man,
> And lead thy thousand horse with my conduct…
>
> Both we shall raigne as Consuls of the earth,
> And mightie kings shall be our Senators…
>
> May we become immortall like the Gods.
>
> (*Tamburlaine the Great*, Act 1, Scene 2, lines 368-372, 83-384, 393-394, 396: 18-19.)

Lewis was concerned about the way Marlowe depicted his protagonist. Unlike Shakespeare, his contemporary, who depicted a mixture of good and bad qualities in such "rounded" characters as Coriolanus*, Julius Caesar*, and Henry the Fifth*, Tamberlaine is a "flat" character, exhibiting only pride and cruelty. He conquers country after country and shows no mercy to the inhabitants who sue for peace. He even kills one of his three sons who lacks the desire to continue his father's ruthless campaigns. Illness brings his life to an end, but Marlowe does not represent it as divine judgment.

Marlowe thus introduced a new type of villain, in the opinion of Lewis. Before *Tamburlaine*, the archetypical story in the medieval mind was a hero like Jack the Giant Killer, who represented the weak but good people who triumph over the strong, bad ones when the odds are against them. But now, "The older type of villain starts up at hero. Tamburlaine is Grendel, Herod, and Giant Blunderbore all in one, but the author seems to me to be on his side.

The play is a hideous moral spoonerism: Giant the Jack Killer" (EL: 52). One of Lewis' students recalls him saying "Marlowe, next to Carlyle, was the most thoroughly depraved of English writers" (Brewer: 49). And Tamburlaine was "Marlowe's lunatic" (PP: 112).

Tamberlaine's pride and ambition reached to the heavens, so to speak, and given the time of his life in the distant past and his moral corruption, he is a logical choice for Lewis to not only place him in Hell, but also at a great distance ("light years") from the bus stop.

Tantalus (Ch 8, p 34)

Once so favored by the gods that he enjoyed their company on Mount Olympus, Tantalus incurred their wrath by bringing ambrosia, the food of the gods, and nectar, their drink, down to mortals down on earth. He was punished by being imprisoned in a pond up to his neck. Branches of a fruit tree hung low over his head, but when he wanted to eat, the wind blew the branches beyond his reach. And every time he tried to drink the waters receded. From his name "tantalize" has entered our language.

Trajan (Ch 9)

Marcus Ulpius Nerva Traianus (September 18, A. D. 53–August 9, 117), Roman Emperor (98-117), commonly known as Trajan. Born in Spain, he rose through the ranks of the army and was adopted as son and successor by Emperor Nerva in 97, a gesture calculated to increase Nerva's popularity with the army. Trajan ruled well, and the empire reached its greatest size under him. The Roman senate gave him the title "Optimus," meaning "The Best."

In the middle ages, many believed that by divine intercession, Pope Gregory I resurrected Trajan and baptized him into the Christian faith. Theologians such as Thomas Aquinas regarded him as a virtuous pagan, and Dante placed his spirit in the sixth Heaven, the Heaven of Jupiter where the just such as David, Constantine and Trajan now contemplate the Divine Essence. Lewis follows Dante in this regard, saying through MacDonald that Trajan did take the bus and stayed in Heaven.

Unicorns (Ch 8, p 34)

Lewis used the white unicorn and many other mythical creatures and gods in his writings because they "were to him abbreviated symbols of qualities present in the world, or as Lewis in one place calls them, 'words of a language which speaks the else unspeakable'" (Hooper, in P: vi).

In his poem "The Late Passenger," as Lewis explained in his correspondence, "The Unicorn, as often in medieval symbolism, is Christ rejected" (CLIII, "To Roger Lancelyn Green (BOD)," April 17, 1958; 936). The reluctance of Noah's sons to admit the unicorn into the ark was a symbol for the world not receiving Christ.

> Oh noble and unmated beast, my sons were all unkind;
> In such a night what stable and what manger will you find? (P: 48)

The unicorns served a very different purpose in regard to the self-conscious woman. They were quite at home in Heaven's stables, and ready to help in any way they could. But Lewis couldn't resist adding a Biblical reference as he wondered "for what real battle it might be the rehearsal" when he sees "how their hind legs went up and their horned heads down in mimic battle" (62). I believe he was recalling John's description of the Second Coming, when Jesus and the armies of Heaven come on white horses (why not unicorns?) to do battle with His enemies (Rev 19:11-16).

Via Dolorosa (Ch 6, p 31)

Latin for "Way of Sorrows," the phrase refers to the path Jesus took through Jerusalem while bearing his cross. Many pilgrims visited Jerusalem over the centuries, and eventually the journey became associated with fourteen "stations" which gave worshippers places to stop and meditate over what Christ endured.

Station 1.   Jesus is condemned to death.

Station 2.   Jesus is given his cross.

Station 3.   Jesus falls the first time.

Station 4.   Jesus meets his mother.

Station 5.   Simon of Cyrene carries the cross for Jesus.

Station 6.   Veronica wipes the face of Jesus.

Station 7.   Jesus falls the second time.

Station 8.   Jesus meets the women of Jerusalem.

Station 9.   Jesus falls the third time.

Station 10. Jesus is stripped of his garments.

Station 11. The Crucifixion.

Station 12. Jesus dies on the Cross.

Station 13. Jesus' body is removed from the cross.

Station 14. Jesus is laid in the tomb and covered with incense.

I hesitate to draw a parallel between Ikey and Jesus, and yet Lewis strongly emphasized Ikey's tremendous exertions that left him lame while "carrying his torture" (51); language that, along with *via dolorosa*, unmistakably recalls the suffering of Jesus who also carried his instrument of torture. But in the end, one atoned for the world and entered Hades, while the tremendous efforts of the other, however well-intended, were in vain.

Virgil (p xix)

Publius Virgilius Maro, generally recognized as the greatest Roman poet, was born in Northern Italy (at that time a region in Gaul) on October 15, 70 and died on September 21, 19 B. C. E. Little is known of his background other than his father was fairly prosperous and was able to afford a good education for Virgil. In addition to the *Aeneid*, Virgil also wrote the *Eclogues*, a series of rustic poems, and the *Georgics* ("pertaining to agriculture"), which described the cultivation of grapes and olives, the raising of livestock, and bee keeping.

After Octavian conquered his rival Antony, he became Rome's first dictator and wore the title of Augustus. He urged Virgil to write the glorious history of Rome under him, and so Virgil spent the rest of his life working on the *Aeneid*. Virgil met Augustus in Athens and accompanied him on the return to Italy, but soon after arriving he died of a fever he had contracted in Greece. He gave instructions to his executor Varius to destroy the incomplete manuscript of the *Aeneid*, but Augustus countermanded the instructions, and the work was eventually published

BIBLIOGRAPHY

Blake, William. *The Marriage of Heaven and Hell.* Introduction by Clark Emery. Critical Studies No. 1. Coral Gables: University of Miami Press, 1963.

Brewer, Derek. "The Tutor: A Portrait," in *C. S. Lewis at the Breakfast Table and Other Reminiscences.* New York: Macmillan, 1979, 41-67.

British currency values for 1900 and 1945 were obtained from measuringworth.com.

Aesop's Fables. New York: Grosset & Dunlap, 1947.

Brooke, C. F. Tucker, ed. *The Works of Christopher Marlowe. Tamburlaine the Greate.* Oxford: At the Clarendon Press, (1910) 1969.

Camps, W. A. *An Introduction to Virgil's* Aeneid. Oxford: Oxford University Press, 1969.

Carroll, Lewis. *Alice's Adventures in Wonderland* and *Through the Looking-Glass.* New York: Grosset and Dunlap, n.d.

Clark, David G. "A Brief Discussion of the Designations for Persons in *The Screwtape Letters. The Lamp-Post of the Southern California C. S. Lewis Society,* Fall-Winter, 2002 (Vol. 26, No. 3-4), 19-29.

Clough, Arthur Hugh. *Poems. With a Memoir.* London: Macmillan and Co., 1879 (7th. ed.)

The Complete Poetical Works and Letters of John Keats. Horace E. Scudder, ed. The Cambridge Edition of the Poets. Boston and New York: Houghton Mifflin Company, 1899.

Cowper, William. *The Correspondence of William Cowper. Arranged in Chronological Order, With Annotations.* Volume IV. Thomas Wright, ed. London: Hodder & Stoughton, 1904.

Danto, Arthur C. *Encounters and Reflections. Art in the Historical Present.* Berkeley: University of California Press, 1997 (1986).

"I Enoch," E. Isaac, Translator. *The Old Testament Pseudepigrapha.* Volume I: *Apocalyptic Literature and Testaments.* Charlesworth, James H., ed. New York: Doubleday, 1983.

Ford, Paul F. *Companion to Narnia. A Complete Guide to the Enchanting World of C. S. Lewis's* The Chronicles of Narnia. Fourth Edition. HarperSanFrancisco, a division of HarperCollins, New York: 1994 (1980).

Goffar, Janine. *C. S. Lewis Index. Rumours from the Sculptor's Shop.* Riverside, CA: La Sierra University Press, 1995.

Gospel of Thomas. Bruce M. Metzger, Trans. *Synopsis Quattuor Evangeliorum.* Stuttgart: Wurttembergische Bibelanstalt, 1968.

Hooper, Walter. *C. S. Lewis. A Companion and Guide.* San Francisco: Harper (an imprint of HarperCollins), 1996.

John Milton. Complete Poems and Major Prose. Merritt Y. Hughes, ed. New York: The Odyssey Press, 1957.

The Comedy of Dante Alighieri, The Florentine. Cantica I: Hell. Dorothy L. Sayers, trans. New York: Penguin Books, 1949.

The Comedy of Dante Alighieri, The Florentine. Cantica II: Purgatory. Dorothy L. Sayers, trans. Baltimore, MD: Penguin Books, 1960 (1955).

The Comedy of Dante Alighieri, The Florentine. Cantica III: Paradise. Dorothy L. Sayers and Barbara Reynolds, trans. New York, NY: Penguin Books, 1962.

Clough, Arthur Hugh. "Say not the Struggle Naught Availeth". www.poemhunter.com

Harris, Wendell V. *Arthur Hugh Clough.* New York: Twayne Publishers, Inc., 1970.

Julian of Norwich, *The Revelation of Divine Love in Sixteen Showings Made to Dame Julian of Norwich.* Translated with a New Introduction by M. L. del Mastro. Ligouri, Missouri: Ligouri/Triumph. An imprint of Ligouri Publications, 1994 (1977).

Khoddam, Salva. "The Enclosed Garden in C. S. Lewis's *The Chronicles of Narnia. The Bulletin of the New York C. S. Lewis Society*, January/February 2006 (Vol. 37, No. 1, Whole No. 411), 1-10.

Lindskoog, Kathryn. "Meeting C. S. Lewis," *The Lamp-Post of the Southern California C. S. Lewis Society*, Summer 2000 (Vol. 24, No. 2), 11-14.

MacDonald, George. *George MacDonald: An Anthology.* Edited and with Introduction by C. S. Lewis. New York: Macmillan, 1974 (1946).

Olson, Stanley. *John Singer Sargent. His Portrait.* New York: St. Martin's Press, 1986.

Owen, George Vale. *The Life Beyond the Veil. Spirit Messages Received and Written Down by the Rev. G. Vale Owen.* Vicar of Orford, Lancashire. With an Appreciation by Lord Northcliffe, and an Introduction by Sir Arthur Conan Doyle, M. D., LL.D. Book I: *The Lowlands of Heaven.* London: Thornton Butterworth Ltd.,

1920. In America: H. W. Engholm, ed. New York: George H. Doran Company, 1921.

The Oxford Classical Dictionary. N. G. L. Hammond and H. H. Scullard, eds. Second Ed. Oxford: At the Clarendon Press, 1970.

The Oxford Dictionary of the Christian Church. F. L. Cross, ed. "Julian of Norwich". London: Oxford University Press, 1958. P. 753.

Paananien, Victor N. *William Blake.* Boston: Twayne Publishers, a Division of G. H. Hall and Co., 1977.

Parker, Deborah. *Commentary and Ideology: Dante in the Renaissance.* Durham: Duke University Press, 1993.

Prettejohn, Elizabeth. *Interpreting Sargent.* New York: Stewart, Tabori & Chang, 1999.

Roberts, Keith. *Cezanne.* New York: Tudor Publishing Co., 1967.

Seitz, William C. *Claude Monet. Seasons and Moments.* New York: Doubleday & Co., Inc., 1960.

Shakespeare, William. *Julius Caesar.* Maurice Charney, ed. The Shakespeare Parallel Text Series. Logan, Iowa: The Perfection Form Company, 1983.

Shakespeare, William. *The Life of King Henry the Fifth.* G. C. Moore Smith, ed. The Arden Shakespeare. Boston: D. C. Heath and Co, 1896.

Shakespeare, William. *The Tragedy of Coriolanus.* Brook, C. F. Tucker, ed. New Haven: Yale University Press, (1924), 1957.

Tacitus on Britain and Germany. H. Mattingly, trans., revised by S. A. Handford. New York: Penguin Putnam, Inc., 1970 (1948).

The Vita Nuova of Dante. Translated with Introduction and Notes by Theodore Martin. London: Parker, Son, and Bourne, West Strand, 1862.

Venturi, Lionello. *Four Steps Toward Modern Art. Giorgione, Caravaggio, Manet, Cezanne.* New York: Columbia University Press, 1956.

C. S. Lewis Goes to Heaven

INDEX

ABOUT THE AUTHOR

PHOTO BY RUPERT VEGA
WWW.PHOTOGRAPHYBYRUPERT.COM

David Clark (Ph.D., University of Notre Dame) is Professor Emeritus at Vanguard University in Southern California and has taught courses in New Testament, the Intertestamental period and apocalyptic literature as well as New Testament Greek and the theology of C.S. Lewis in both graduate and undergraduate programs. He is the former senior editor of *The Lamp-Post, The Journal of the Southern California C.S. Lewis Society* and the author of *C.S. Lewis: A Guide to His Theology*, (Blackwell, 2007). Dr. Clark especially enjoys working with graduate students as they develop their theses and directed readings for presentation.

OTHER BOOKS OF INTEREST

C. S. Lewis

C. S. Lewis: Views From Wake Forest - Essays on C. S. Lewis
Michael Travers, editor

Contains sixteen scholarly presentations from the international C. S. Lewis convention
in Wake Forest, NC. Walter Hooper shares his important essay "Editing C. S. Lewis," a
chronicle of publishing decisions after Lewis' death in 1963.

*"Scholars from a variety of disciplines address a wide range of issues. The happy result is a fresh and
expansive view of an author who well deserves this kind of thoughtful attention."*
Diana Pavlac Glyer, author of *The Company They Keep*

The Hidden Story of Narnia:
A Book-By-Book Guide to Lewis' Spiritual Themes
Will Vaus

A book of insightful commentary equally suited for teens or adults – Will Vaus points out
connections between the *Narnia* books and spiritual/biblical themes, as well as between
ideas in the *Narnia* books and C. S. Lewis' other books. Learn what Lewis himself said
about the overarching and unifying thematic structure of the Narnia books. That is what this
book explores; what C. S. Lewis called "the hidden story" of Narnia. Each chapter includes
questions for individual use or small group discussion.

Why I Believe in Narnia:
33 Reviews and Essays on the Life and Work of C.S. Lewis
James Como

Chapters range from reviews of critical books , documentaries and movies to evaluations of
Lewis' books to biographical analysis.
*"A valuable, wide-ranging collection of essays by one of the best informed and most accute commentators
on Lewis' work and ideas."*
Peter Schakel, author of *Imagination & the Arts in C.S. Lewis*

Shadows and Chivalry:
C.S. Lewis and George MacDonald on Suffering, Evil, and Death
Jeff McInnis

Shadows and Chivalry studies the influence of George MacDonald, a nineteenth-century
Scottish novelist and fantasy writer, upon one of the most influential writers of modern times,
C. S. Lewis—the creator of Narnia, literary critic, and best-selling apologist. This study
attempts to trace the overall affect of MacDonald's work on Lewis's thought and imagination.
Without ever ceasing to be a story of one man's influence upon another, the study also serves
as an exploration of each writer's thought on, and literary visions of, good and evil.

C. S. Lewis & Philosophy as a Way of Life: His Philosophical Thoughts
Adam Barkman

C. S. Lewis is rarely thought of as a "philosopher" per se despite having both studied and taught philosophy for several years at Oxford. Lewis's long journey to Christianity was essentially philosophical – passing through seven different stages. This 624 page book is an invaluable reference for C. S. Lewis scholars and fans alike

C. S. Lewis: His Literary Achievement
Colin Manlove

"This is a positively brilliant book, written with splendor, elegance, profundity and evidencing an enormous amount of learning. This is probably not a book to give a first-time reader of Lewis. But for those who are more broadly read in the Lewis corpus this book is an absolute gold mine of information. The author gives us a magnificent overview of Lewis' many writings, tracing for us thoughts and ideas which recur throughout, and at the same time telling us how each book differs from the others. I think it is not extravagant to call C. S. Lewis: His Literary Achievement a tour de force."

Robert Merchant, *St. Austin Review*, Book Review Editor

Mythopoeic Narnia: Memory, Metaphor, and Metamorphoses in C. S. Lewis's The Chronicles of Narnia
Salwa Khoddam

Dr. Khoddam, the founder of the C. S. Lewis and Inklings Society (2004), has been teaching university courses using Lewis' books for over 25 years. Her book offers a fresh approach to the *Narnia* books based on an inquiry into Lewis' readings and use of classical and Christian symbols. She explores the literary and intellectual contexts of these stories, the traditional myths and motifs, and places them in the company of the greatest Christian mythopoeic works of Western Literature. In Lewis' imagination, memory and metaphor interact to advance his purpose – a Christian metamorphosis. *Mythopoeic Narnia* helps to open the door for readers into the magical world of the Western imagination.

Speaking of Jack: A C. S. Lewis Discussion Guide
Will Vaus

C. S. Lewis Societies have been forming around the world since the first one started in New York City in 1969. Will Vaus has started and led three groups himself. *Speaking of Jack* is the result of Vaus' experience in leading those Lewis Societies. Included here are introductions to most of Lewis' books as well as questions designed to stimulate discussion about Lewis' life and work. These materials have been "road-tested" with real groups made up of young and old, some very familiar with Lewis and some newcomers. *Speaking of Jack* may be used in an existing book discussion group, to start a C. S. Lewis Society, or as a guide to your own exploration of Lewis' books.

George MacDonald

Diary of an Old Soul & The White Page Poems
George MacDonald and Betty Aberlin

The first edition of George MacDonald's book of daily poems included a blank page opposite each page of poems. Readers were invited to write their own reflections on the "white page." MacDonald wrote: "Let your white page be ground, my print be seed, growing to golden ears, that faith and hope may feed." Betty Aberlin responded to MacDonald's invitation with daily poems of her own.

Betty Aberlin's close readings of George MacDonald's verses and her thoughtful responses to them speak clearly of her poetic gifts and spiritual intelligence.
    Luci Shaw, poet

George MacDonald: Literary Heritage and Heirs
Roderick McGillis, editor

This latest collection of 14 essays sets a new standard that will influence MacDonald studies for many more years. George MacDonald experts are increasingly evaluating his entire corpus within the nineteenth century context.

This comprehensive collection represents the best of contemporary scholarship on George MacDonald.
    Rolland Hein, author of *George MacDonald: Victorian Mythmaker*

In the Near Loss of Everything: George MacDonald's Son in America
Dale Wayne Slusser

In the summer of 1887, George MacDonald's son Ronald, newly engaged to artist Louise Blandy, sailed from England to America to teach school. The next summer he returned to England to marry Louise and bring her back to America. On August 27, 1890, Louise died leaving him with an infant daughter. Ronald once described losing a beloved spouse as "the near loss of everything". Dale Wayne Slusser unfolds this poignant story with unpublished letters and photos that give readers a glimpse into the close-knit MacDonald family. Also included is Ronald's essay about his father, *George MacDonald: A Personal Note*, plus a selection from Ronald's 1922 fable, *The Laughing Elf*, about the necessity of both sorrow and joy in life.

A Novel Pulpit: Sermons From George MacDonald's Fiction
David L. Neuhouser

"MacDonald's novels are both stimulating and thought-provoking. This collection of sermons from ten novels serve to bring out the 'freshness and brilliance' of MacDonald's message."
    from the author's introduction

Behind the Back of the North Wind: Essays on George MacDonald's Classic Book
Edited and with Introduction by John Pennington and Roderick McGillis

The unique blend of fairy tale atmosphere and social realism in this novel laid the groundwork for modern fantasy literature. Sixteen essays by various authors are accompanied by an instructive introduction, extensive index,and beautiful illustrations.

Pop Culture

To Love Another Person: A Spiritual Journey Through Les Miserables
John Morrison

The powerful story of Jean Valjean's redemption is beloved by readers and theater goers everywhere. In this companion and guide to Victor Hugo's masterpiece, author John Morrison unfolds the spiritual depth and breadth of this classic novel and broadway musical.

Through Common Things: Philosophical Reflections on Popular Culture
Adam Barkman

"Barkman presents us with an amazingly wide-ranging collection of philosophical reflections grounded in the everyday things of popular culture – past and present, eastern and western, factual and fictional. Throughout his encounters with often surprising subject-matter (the value of darkness?), he writes clearly and concisely, moving seamlessly between Aristotle and anime, Lord Buddha and Lord Voldemort.... . This is an informative and entertaining book to read!"
Doug Bloomberg, Professor of Philosophy, Institute for Christian Studies

Spotlight:
A Close-up Look at the Artistry and Meaning of Stephenie Meyer's Twilight Novels
John Granger

Stephenie Meyer's *Twilight* saga has taken the world by storm. But is there more to *Twilight* than a love story for teen girls crossed with a cheesy vampire-werewolf drama? *Spotlight* reveals the literary backdrop, themes, artistry, and meaning of the four Bella Swan adventures. *Spotlight* is the perfect gift for serious *Twilight* readers.

Virtuous Worlds: The Video Gamer's Guide to Spiritual Truth
John Stanifer

Popular titles like *Halo 3* and *The Legend of Zelda: Twilight Princess* fly off shelves at a mind-blowing rate. John Stanifer, an avid gamer, shows readers specific parallels between Christian faith and the content of their favorite games. Written with wry humor (including a heckler who frequently pokes fun at the author) this book will appeal to gamers and non-gamers alike. Those unfamiliar with video games may be pleasantly surprised to find that many elements in those "virtual worlds" also qualify them as "virtuous worlds."

Memoir

Called to Serve: Life as a Firefighter-Deacon
Deacon Anthony R. Surozenski

Called to Serve is the story of one man's dream to be a firefighter. But dreams have a way of taking detours – so Tony Soruzenski became a teacher and eventually a volunteer firefighter. And when God enters the picture, Tony is faced with a choice. Will he give up firefighting to follow another call? After many years, Tony's two callings are finally united – in service as a fire chaplain at Ground Zero after the 9-11 attacks and in other ways he could not have imagined. Tony is Chief Chaplain's aid for the Massachusettes Corp of Fire Chaplains and Director for the Office of the Diaconate of the Diocese of Worcester, Massachusettes.

Harry Potter

The Order of Harry Potter: The Literary Skill of the Hogwarts Epic
Colin Manlove

Colin Manlove, a popular conference speaker and author of over a dozen books, has earned an international reputation as an expert on fantasy and children's literature. His book, *From Alice to Harry Potter*, is a survey of 400 English fantasy books. In *The Order of Harry Potter*, he compares and contrasts *Harry Potter* with works by "Inklings" writers J.R.R. Tolkien, C.S. Lewis and Charles Williams; he also examines Rowling's treatment of the topic of imagination; her skill in organization and the use of language; and the book's underlying motifs and themes.

Harry Potter & Imagination: The Way Between Two Worlds
Travis Prinzi

Imaginative literature places a reader between two worlds: the story world and the world of daily life, and challenges the reader to imagine and to act for a better world. Starting with discussion of Harry Potter's more important themes, *Harry Potter & Imagination* takes readers on a journey through the transformative power of those themes for both the individual and for culture by placing Rowling's series in its literary, historical, and cultural contexts.

Repotting Harry Potter: A Professor's Guide for the Serious Re-Reader
Rowling Revisited: Return Trips to Harry, Fantastic Beasts, Quidditch, & Beedle the Bard
Dr. James W. Thomas

In *Repotting Harry Potter* and his sequel book *Rowling Revisited*, Dr. James W. Thomas points out the humor, puns, foreshadowing and literary parallels in the Potter books. In *Rowling Revisted*, readers will especially find useful three extensive appendixes – "Fantastic Beasts and the Pages Where You'll Find Them," "Quidditch Through the Pages," and "The Books in the Potter Books." Dr. Thomas makes re-reading the Potter books even more rewarding and enjoyable.

Deathly Hallows Lectures:
The Hogwarts Professor Explains Harry's Final Adventure
John Granger

In *The Deathly Hallows Lectures*, John Granger reveals the finale's brilliant details, themes, and meanings. *Harry Potter* fans will be surprised by and delighted with Granger's explanations of the three dimensions of meaning in *Deathly Hallows*. Ms. Rowling has said that alchemy sets the "parameters of magic" in the series; after reading the chapter-length explanation of *Deathly Hallows* as the final stage of the alchemical Great Work, the serious reader will understand how important literary alchemy is in understanding Rowling's artistry and accomplishment.

Hog's Head Conversations: Essays on Harry Potter
Travis Prinzi, Editor

Ten fascinating essays on Harry Potter by popular Potter writers and speakers including John Granger, James W. Thomas, Colin Manlove, and Travis Prinzi.

Poets and Poetry

Remembering Roy Campbell: The Memoirs of his Daughters, Anna and Tess
Introduction by Judith Lütge Coullie, Editor
Preface by Joseph Pearce

Anna and Teresa Campbell were the daughters of the handsome young South African poet and writer, Roy Campbell (1901-1957), and his beautiful English wife, Mary Garman. In their frank and moving memoirs, Anna and Tess recall the extraordinary, and often very difficult, lives they shared with their exceptional parents. Over 50 photos, 344 footnotes, timeline of Campbell's life, and complete index.

In the Eye of the Beholder: How to See the World Like a Romantic Poet
Louis Markos

Born out of the French Revolution and its radical faith that a nation could be shaped and altered by the dreams and visions of its people, British Romantic Poetry was founded on a belief that the objects and realities of our world, whether natural or human, are not fixed in stone but can be molded and transformed by the visionary eye of the poet. Unlike many of the books written on Romanticism, which devote many pages to the poets and few pages to their poetry, the focus here is firmly on the poems themselves. The author thereby draws the reader intimately into the life of these poems. A separate bibliographical essay is provided for readers listing accessible biographies of each poet and critical studies of their work.

The Cat on the Catamaran: A Christmas Tale
John Martin

Here is a modern-day parable of a modern-day cat with modern-day attitudes. Riverboat Dan is a "cool" cat on a perpetual vacation from responsibility. He's *The Cat on the Catamaran* – sailing down the river of life. Dan keeps his guilty conscience from interfering with his fun until he runs into trouble. But will he have the courage to believe that it's never too late to change course? (For ages 10 to adult)

"Cat lovers and poetry lovers alike will enjoy this whimsical story about Riverboat Dan, a philosophical cat in search of meaning."
    Regina Doman, author of *Angel in the Water*

Fiction

The Iona Conspiracy (from The Remnant Chronicles book series)
Gary Gregg

Readers find themselves on a modern adventure through ancient Celtic myth and legend as thirteen year old Jacob uncovers his destiny within "the remnant" of the Sporrai Order. As the Iona Academy comes under the control of educational reformers and ideological scientists, Jacob finds himself on a dangerous mission to the sacred Scottish island of Iona and discovers how his life is wrapped up with the fate of the long lost cover of *The Book of Kells*. From its connections to Arthurian legend to references to real-life people, places, and historical mysteries, *Iona* is an adventure that speaks to eternal truths as well as the challenges of the modern world. A young adult novel, *Iona* can be enjoyed by the entire family.

CPSIA information can be obtained at www.ICGtesting.com
Printed in the USA
LVOW111239101012

302247LV00004B/47/P